917. 4461.

I0656315

Pocket
BOSTON
TOP SIGHTS • LOCAL LIFE • MADE EASY

Gregor Clark

In This Book

QuickStart Guide

Your keys to understanding the city – we help you decide what to do and how to do it

Need to Know
Tips for a smooth trip

Neighborhoods
What's where

Explore Boston

The best things to see and do, neighborhood by neighborhood

Top Sights
Make the most of your visit

Local Life
The insider's city

The Best of Boston

The city's highlights in handy lists to help you plan

Best Walks
See the city on foot

Boston's Best...
The best experiences

Survival Guide

Tips and tricks for a seamless, hassle-free city experience

Getting Around
Travel like a local

Essential Information
Including where to stay

Our selection of the city's best places to eat, drink and experience:

◉ **Sights**

✖ **Eating**

🍷 **Drinking**

✪ **Entertainment**

🔒 **Shopping**

These symbols give you the vital information for each listing:

📞 Telephone Numbers
🕑 Opening Hours
P Parking
🚭 Nonsmoking
@ Internet Access
📶 Wi-Fi Access
🥗 Vegetarian Selection
📖 English-Language Menu

👪 Family-Friendly
🐾 Pet-Friendly
🚌 Bus
⛴ Ferry
T Metro
S Subway
🚋 Tram
🚆 Train

Find each listing quickly on maps for each neighborhood:

Bar Hemingway

16 🍷 Map p233, B2

Legend has it that Hemi self, wielding a machine rate this timber-pan ered bar during showpiece is a en by Papa ar town. Dress s.com; Hôtel Rit ; 🕑6.30pm-2a

Lonely Planet's Boston

Lonely Planet Pocket Guides are designed to get you straight to the heart of the city.

Inside you'll find all the must-see sights, plus tips to make your visit to each one really memorable. We've split the city into easy-to-navigate neighborhoods and provided clear maps so you'll find your way around with ease. Our expert authors have searched out the best of the city: walks, food, nightlife and shopping, to name a few. Because you want to explore, our 'Local Life' pages will take you to some of the most exciting areas to experience the real Boston.

And of course you'll find all the practical tips you need for a smooth trip: itineraries for short visits, how to get around, and how much to tip the guy who serves you a drink at the end of a long day's exploration.

It's your guarantee of a really great experience.

Our Promise

You can trust our travel information because Lonely Planet authors visit the places we write about, each and every edition. We never accept freebies for positive coverage, so you can rely on us to tell it like it is.

QuickStart Guide 7

Boston Top Sights.................. 8

Boston Local Life 12

Boston Day Planner.......... 14

Need to Know..................... 16

Boston Neighborhoods...... 18

Explore Boston 21

22 Charlestown

30 West End & North End

44 Beacon Hill & Boston Common

56 Downtown & the Waterfront..

76 South End & Chinatown

88 Back Bay

104 Kenmore Square & Fenway

116 Cambridge

Worth a Trip:

Boston Harbor Islands................... 72

The Best of Boston 129

Boston's Best Walks

Freedom Trail ... **130**

Green Spaces &
Shopping Places ... **134**

Boston's Best ...

Eating ... **136**

Drinking ... **138**

Entertainment ... **140**

Shopping ... **141**

For Kids ... **142**

Museums ... **144**

Spectator Sports ... **145**

For Free ... **146**

History ... **147**

Tours ... **148**

Survival Guide 149

Before You Go ... **150**

When to Go ... **150**

Book Your Stay ... **150**

Arriving in Boston ... **151**

Getting Around ... **151**

Essential Information ... **152**

QuickStart Guide

Welcome to Boston

Boston's winding streets recall revolution and renewal; even today, this is a forward-thinking and barrier-breaking city. Though you can hardly walk a step without running into some historic site, Boston remains vital, with vibrant artistic scenes, cutting-edge urban planning, and ever-present scholars and thinkers shaping the evolving culture.

Old North Church (p36), North End
HDNRG/SHUTTERSTOCK ©

Boston
Top Sights

Museum of Fine Arts (p106)

Eclectic, encyclopedic art museum.

Trinity Church
(p92)

Architect Henry Hobson
Richardson's crowning
achievement.

Fenway Park (p110)

America's oldest major-
league baseball stadium.

New England Aquarium (p58)

Superb aquarium with a three-story ocean tank.

Institute of Contemporary Art (p60)

Pioneer of Boston's thriving art scene.

Boston Harbor Islands (p72)

National park comprising 34 islands.

Harvard Yard (p118)

Historic heart of Harvard University.

Boston Public Library (p90)

A treasure trove of beautiful works.

Charlestown Navy Yard (p24)

Home to the storied USS *Constitution*.

Isabella Stewart Gardner Museum (p108)

Exquisite art in a magnificent building.

Boston Common (p46)

America's oldest public park.

Boston Local Life

Local experiences and hidden gems
to help you uncover the real city

It's no secret that Boston is rich in historic sites and cultural institutions, but it's also a city of dynamic neighborhoods and local people. Here's your introduction to the city's ethnic enclaves, art markets, local boutiques and student hangouts.

Italian Culture in the North End (p32)
☑ Irresistible food and drink ☑ Old-world ambience

South End Art Stroll (p78)
☑ Local artists ☑ Victorian architecture

Back Bay Fashion Walk (p94)
☑ Trendy boutiques ☑ Local design

Other great places to experience the city like a local:

Drinking in the North End (p40)

Hidden Beacon Hill (p53)

The Lawn on D (p71)

Charles River Esplanade (p98)

Food trucks (p125)

Zume's Coffee House (p29)

21st Amendment (p54)

Lucky's Lounge (p70)

Delux Café (p84)

Trident Booksellers (p100)

CAMBRIDGE SAVINGS BANK

CAMBRIDGE VISITOR'S INFORMATION CENTER

Offbeat Harvard Square (p120)
☑ Bookstores and buskers ☑ Coffee shops

Boston
Day Planner

Day One

Spend your first day in Boston following the **Freedom Trail** (p130), which starts on the **Boston Common** (p46) and continues through downtown. You won't have time to go inside every museum, but you can admire the architecture and learn the history. Highlights include the **Old South Meeting House** (p64), the **Old State House** (p64) and **Faneuil Hall** (p65). Grab lunch from one of the many eateries in **Quincy Market** (p68).

In the afternoon, the Freedom Trail continues into the North End, where you can visit the historic **Paul Revere House** (p36), **Old North Church** (p36) and **Copp's Hill Burying Ground** (p36). In Charlestown, tour the **USS Constitution** (p25) and climb the **Bunker Hill Monument** (p27).

For dinner, you are perfectly poised for an Italian feast along Hanover St, perhaps at **Pomodoro** (p38) or **Giacomo's Ristorante** (p39). Afterward, head for the former Charles St Jail – now the exquisite Liberty Hotel – where you can sip cocktails under the soaring lobby or head down to the former 'drunk tank,' which now houses the ultracool club **Alibi** (p40).

Day Two

Spend the morning exploring Boston's most architecturally significant collection of buildings, clustered around Copley Sq. Admire the art and books at the **Boston Public Library** (p90) and ogle the magnificent stained-glass windows at **Trinity Church** (p92). For lunch, treat yourself to some fine seafood at **Atlantic Fish Co** (p99).

Your afternoon is reserved for one of Boston's magnificent art museums. Unfortunately, you'll have to choose between the excellent, encyclopedic collection at the **Museum of Fine Arts** (p106) or the smaller but no less extraordinary exhibits at the **Isabella Stewart Gardner Museum** (p108). Either way, you won't be disappointed.

In the evening head to **Fenway Park** (p110) to see the Red Sox play baseball. If you're not lucky enough to score tickets, hang out at the **Bleacher Bar** (p114) to sneak a peek inside the ball park. If sports aren't your thing, you might prefer a performance by the world-class **Boston Symphony Orchestra** (p115), which takes place in the same neighborhood.

Short on time?
We've arranged Boston's must-sees into these day-by-day itineraries to make sure you see the very best of the city in the time you have available.

Day Three

Rent a bicycle and spend the morning cycling along the **Charles River Esplanade** (p98). Cross the river to Cambridge for scenic views of scullers and sailboats on the Charles, with the Boston city skyline as the backdrop.

While away the afternoon in Harvard Sq, browsing the bookstores and cruising the cafes, or catch a free tour of **Harvard Yard** (p118).

Don't miss the chance to see whatever brilliant or bizarre production is playing at the **American Repertory Theater** (p127). If that doesn't take your fancy, go for drinks and live music at **Club Passim** (p126) or **Sinclair** (p127).

Day Four

Spend the morning on the water, either on a **whale-watching tour** (p66) to Stellwagen Bank or a trip to the **Boston Harbor Islands** (p73). Alternatively, get a closer view of the marine life inside the **New England Aquarium** (p58).

Afterward, stroll along the HarborWalk and into the Seaport District, admiring the harbor views along the way. Have lunch with a view at **Legal Harborside** (p67), or super-fresh seafood at **Yankee Lobster Co** (p67). Continue to the **Institute of Contemporary Art** (p60) for an afternoon of provocative contemporary art. Don't miss the amazing view from the Founders Gallery.

In the evening explore the trendsetting South End, finishing your evening with cocktails and live jazz at the **Beehive** (p84).

Need to Know

For more information,
see Survival Guide (p149)

Currency
US dollar ($)

Language
English

Visas
Citizens of most countries are eligible for the Visa Waiver Program, which requires prior electronic approval via Electronic System for Travel Authorization (ESTA).

Money
ATMs widely available. Credit cards accepted at most hotels, restaurants and shops.

Cell Phones
Most US cell-phone systems work on the GSM 850/1900 standard, as opposed to the GSM 900/1800 standard used throughout Europe, Australia and Asia.

Time
Eastern Standard Time
(GMT/UTC minus five hours)

Tipping
Tip at least 15% (more for good service) in all bars and restaurants.

① Before You Go

Your Daily Budget

Budget: Less than $100
▶ Dorm bed $50
▶ Pizza or dumplings $5–10
▶ Certain museum nights and walking tours are free
▶ Ride on the T (metro) $2.25–2.75

Midrange: $100–350
▶ Double room in a midrange hotel $100–250
▶ Meal at a midrange restaurant $15–25
▶ Museum admission $15–25
▶ Short taxi ride $15–20

Top end: More than $350
▶ Double room in a top-end hotel from $250
▶ Meal at a top-end restaurant from $25
▶ Gigs, events and other activities from $50

Useful Websites

Lonely Planet (www.lonelyplanet.com/usa/boston) Destination information, hotel bookings, traveler forum and more.

My Secret Boston (www.mysecretboston.com) Food, nightlife, cultural and family events.

Greater Boston Convention & Visitors Bureau (www.bostonusa.com) The official guide to what to do and where to stay.

Advance Planning

One month before Reserve a place to stay. Budget travelers, this means you!

Two weeks before Buy tickets for the Boston Symphony Orchestra or the Red Sox.

One week before Make your dinner reservations.

2 Arriving in Boston

Most visitors will arrive at Logan International Airport, or by train or bus at South Station. Both are easily accessible by subway (metro) trains, better known as the 'T,' operated by the Massachusetts Bay Transportation Authority (MBTA).

From Logan Airport

Destination	Best Transport
Back Bay	Blue line to green line T
Beacon Hill	Silver line bus to red line T
Cambridge	Silver line bus to red line T
Chinatown	Silver line bus
Downtown & Waterfront	Blue line T or silver line bus
Kenmore Sq & Fenway	Blue line to green line T
West End & North End	Blue line to green or orange line T

From South Station

Destination	Best Transport
Back Bay	Red line to green line T
Beacon Hill	Red line T
Cambridge	Red line T
Chinatown	Walk
Downtown & Waterfront	Walk
Kenmore Sq & Fenway	Red line to green line T
West End & North End	Red line to green or orange line T

3 Getting Around

Boston is a wonderful walking or cycling city. Otherwise, most of the main attractions are accessible by the 'T'. Bus and T fares are slightly cheaper if you use a plastic 'Charlie Card,' which is available at any station.

T Metro (the T)

The MBTA (www.mbta.com) operates the USA's oldest subway, built in 1897 and known locally as the T, which will take you almost anywhere you want to go in Boston.

Bus

The MBTA operates many bus routes within the city. The silver line is a 'rapid' bus that is useful for Logan Airport (SL1) and the South End (SL4 or SL5).

Bicycle (Hubway)

Boston's bike-share program is the **Hubway** (www.thehubway.com). There are 185 Hubway stations around Boston, Cambridge, Brookline and Somerville, stocked with 1600 bikes that are available for short-term loan. Purchase a temporary membership at any bicycle kiosk, then pay by the half-hour for bike use (free under 30 minutes). Return the bike to any station in the vicinity of your destination.

Boston Neighborhoods
Neighbourhoods

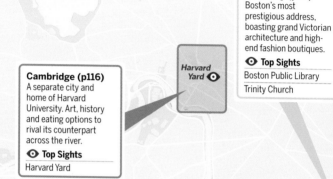

Back Bay (p88)
Boston's most prestigious address, boasting grand Victorian architecture and high-end fashion boutiques.

⊙ **Top Sights**

Boston Public Library

Trinity Church

Cambridge (p116)
A separate city and home of Harvard University. Art, history and eating options to rival its counterpart across the river.

⊙ **Top Sights**

Harvard Yard

Harvard Yard ⊙

Kenmore Square & Fenway (p104)
Home to institutions including the Museum of Fine Arts, the Boston Symphony Orchestra and Fenway Park.

⊙ **Top Sights**

Museum of Fine Arts

Isabella Stewart Gardner Museum

Fenway Park

Fenway ⊙
Park

Isabella Stewart Gardner Museum ⊙ ⊙ Museum of Fine Arts

Worth a Trip

⊙ **Top Sights**

Boston Harbor Islands (p72)

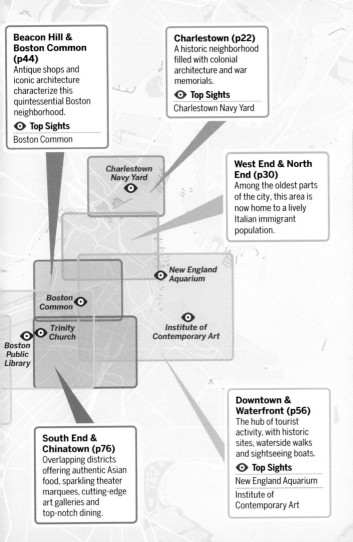

Beacon Hill & Boston Common (p44)
Antique shops and iconic architecture characterize this quintessential Boston neighborhood.

◉ **Top Sights**
Boston Common

Charlestown (p22)
A historic neighborhood filled with colonial architecture and war memorials.

◉ **Top Sights**
Charlestown Navy Yard

West End & North End (p30)
Among the oldest parts of the city, this area is now home to a lively Italian immigrant population.

Charlestown Navy Yard
◉

New England Aquarium
◉

Boston Common ◉

◉ *Trinity Church*

◉ *Boston Public Library*

◉ *Institute of Contemporary Art*

Downtown & Waterfront (p56)
The hub of tourist activity, with historic sites, waterside walks and sightseeing boats.

◉ **Top Sights**
New England Aquarium
Institute of Contemporary Art

South End & Chinatown (p76)
Overlapping districts offering authentic Asian food, sparkling theater marquees, cutting-edge art galleries and top-notch dining.

Explore
Boston

Charlestown.............................. 22

West End & North End.............. 30

Beacon Hill & Boston Common.. 44

Downtown & the Waterfront...... 56

South End & Chinatown............. 76

Back Bay..................................... 88

Kenmore Square & Fenway......... 104

Cambridge................................... 116

Worth a Trip
Boston Harbor Islands.............................. 72

Downtown Boston (p56) at dusk
SEAN PAVONE/SHUTTERSTOCK ©

Explore

Charlestown

The site of the original settlement of the Massachusetts Bay Colony, Charlestown is the terminus for the Freedom Trail. Many tourists tromp across these historic cobblestone sidewalks to admire the USS *Constitution* and climb to the top of the Bunker Hill Monument, which towers above the neighborhood.

The Sights in a Day

☼ Walk across the Charlestown bridge from North Station, or catch the ferry from Long Wharf, to arrive at the Charlestown waterfront. Your first stop is the **Charlestown Navy Yard** (p24), including a film at the visitor center, a tour of the **USS Constitution** (p25) and a few hours investigating the **USS Constitution Museum** (p25). Take a detour from the Freedom Trail to have lunch at **Pier Six** (p29), with amazing views of the Boston Harbor and city skyline.

☼ After lunch, stroll inland to explore the neighborhood's aged narrow streets, lined with 19th-century Federal and colonial houses, and make your way to the **Bunker Hill Monument** (p27). Get a history lesson at the **Bunker Hill Museum** (p27), then climb to the top of the obelisk for panoramic views.

☾ In the evening make a reservation for dinner at the delightful **Navy Yard Bistro & Wine Bar** (p28).

Top Sights

 Charlestown Navy Yard (p24)

💜 Best of Boston

Drinking
Pier Six (p29)

History
Warren Tavern (p29)

For Free
Charlestown Navy Yard (p24)

Bunker Hill Monument (p27)

USS Constitution Museum (p25)

Getting There

⚓ **Boat** The Massachusetts Bay Transportation Company (MBTA) runs the Inner Harbor Ferry every 15 to 30 minutes between the Charlestown Navy Yard and Long Wharf on the Boston waterfront.

🚌 **Bus** Bus 93 runs between Haymarket and Charlestown every 20 minutes.

Ⓣ **Metro** The closest T stations are Community College (orange line) and North Station (orange and green lines), both a 20-minute walk from the Charlestown sights.

Top Sights
Charlestown Navy Yard

No longer operational, the Charlestown Navy Yard is an architectural and historical monument to the US Navy and its vessels. The oldest commissioned US Navy ship, the USS *Constitution*, has been moored here since 1897. Another formidable warship, the USS *Cassin Young*, also docks here. There's an excellent museum dedicated to the USS *Constitution* and more general naval history. The rest of the shipyard remembers the shipbuilding industry's history.

Map p26, C3

www.nps.gov/bost

admission free

visitor center 9am-5pm Tue-Sun May-Sep, 1-5pm Thu-Sun Oct-Apr

93 from Haymarket, Inner Harbor Ferry from Long Wharf, T North Station

USS *Constitution*

USS Constitution

'Her sides are made of iron!' cried a crewman as he watched a shot bounce off the thick oak hull of the **USS Constitution** (www.oldironsides.com; ⏱2:30-6pm Tue-Fri, 10am-6pm Sat & Sun mid-Apr–Sep, shorter hours Nov–mid-Apr; 🚻) during the War of 1812. This earned the legendary ship her nickname, 'Old Ironsides.' Indeed, she has never gone down in a battle and is still the oldest commissioned US Navy ship, dating to 1797. Fresh off a stem-to-stern restoration in 2017, the ship is open again for tours and looking sharper than ever.

USS Constitution Museum

For a play-by-play account of the various battles of the USS *Constitution*, head to the **USS Constitution Museum** (www.ussconstitutionmuseum.org; suggested donation adult $5-10, child $3-5; ⏱9am-6pm Apr-Oct, 10am-5pm Nov-Mar; 🚻). Especially interesting are the exhibits on the War of 1812 and the Barbary War, which trace the birth of the US Navy during these relatively unknown conflicts. Upstairs, kids can experience what it was like to be a sailor on the USS *Constitution* in 1812.

USS Cassin Young

A formidable example of a Fletcher-class destroyer (a WWII craft that was the Navy's fastest, most versatile ship at the time) **USS Cassin Young** (⏱10am-4pm late May-early Nov) participated in the 1944 Battle of Leyte Gulf, as well as the 1945 invasion of Okinawa. Here, the ship sustained two kamikaze hits, leaving 23 crew members dead and many more wounded. Take a free 45-minute tour, or wander around the main deck on your own.

☑ Top Tips

▸ A free, 10-minute introductory film about the Charlestown Navy Yard is shown throughout the day at the National Park Service (NPS) Visitors Center.

▸ All visitors over the age of 18 must show a photo ID to board the USS *Constitution*.

▸ Navy personnel give guided tours of the ship's top deck, gun deck and cramped quarters (last tour: 5:30pm in summer, 3:30pm in winter). You can also wander around the top deck by yourself, but access is limited.

✕ Take a Break

Stroll east along the waterfront for lunch with a view at Pier Six (p29).

There are also a few restaurants and cafes (including an ice-cream place) at City Sq, a half-mile southwest of the Navy Yard.

Pier 8

Pier 7

Pier 6

Pier 5

Pier 4

Thirteenth St

Ninth St

First Ave

Fourth Ave

Eighth St

Shipyard Park

7

MBTA Inner Harbor Ferry (F4)

Pier 3

Pier 2

Pier 1

Boston Inner Harbor

Decatur St

Third Ave

Sixth St

3

Fifth St

Chelsea St

Lowney St

Second Ave

Bunker Hill St

CHARLESTOWN

Lexington St

Tremont St

Prospect St

Mt Vernon St

Mt Vernon Ave

Chestnut St

Adams St

Putnam St

Charlestown Navy Yard

Constitution Rd

Northern Expwy

Winthrop Square

Park St

Bartlett St

Cross St

Cedar St

Green St

High St

Monument Square

1

Bunker Hill Monument

2

Bunker Hill Museum

Winthrop St

Monument Ave

Pleasant St

Soley St

Cordis St

4

5 Main St

Warren St

6

Prescott St

City Square

Paul Revere Park

Charles River

N Washington S

Elm St

Wood St

Austin St

Community College (0.2mi)

Union St

Devens St

Harvard St

Rutherford Ave

Zakim Bridge

93

1

NORTH END

For reviews see

Top Sights	p24
Sights	p27
Eating	p28
Drinking	p29

200 m
0.1 miles

JORGE SALCEDO/SHUTTERSTOCK ©

Bunker Hill Monument

Sights

Bunker Hill Monument MONUMENT

1 ◉ Map p26, B1

This 220ft granite obelisk monument
commemorates the turning-point
battle that was fought on the surrounding hillside on June 17, 1775.
The Redcoats prevailed, but they lost
more than one-third of their forces,
while the colonists suffered relatively
few casualties. Climb the 294 steps
to the top of the monument to enjoy
the panorama of the city, the harbor
and the North Shore. (www.nps.gov/bost;
Monument Sq; admission free; ⊙9am-5pm
May-Sep, 1-5pm Oct-Apr; 🚌93 from Haymarket, Ⓣ Community College)

Bunker Hill Museum MUSEUM

2 ◉ Map p26, B2

Opposite the Bunker Hill Monument,
this redbrick museum contains two
floors of exhibits, including historical
dioramas, a few artifacts and an

☑ Top Tip

Climbing Bunker Hill

From April to June – due to the in-
flux of school groups – you'll need
a climbing pass before ascending
the Bunker Hill Monument. Passes
are available on a first-come,
first-served basis at the Bunker Hill
Museum (p27).

impressive 360-degree mural depicting the battle. If you can find where the artist signed his masterpiece, you win a prize. (www.nps.gov/bost; 43 Monument Sq; admission free; ⏱9am-5pm May-Sep, 1-5pm Oct-Apr; 🚌93 from Haymarket, 🇹Community College)

Eating

Navy Yard Bistro & Wine Bar   FRENCH $$

3 🍴 Map p26, D2

Dark and romantic, this hideaway is tucked into an off-street pedestrian walkway, allowing for comfortable outdoor seating in summer months. Inside, the cozy, carved-wood interior is an ideal date destination – perfect for roasted quail or braised short ribs and other old-fashioned favorites. The menu also features seasonal

vegetables and excellent wines. (www.navyyardbistro.com; cnr Second Ave & Sixth St; mains $18-36; ⏱4:30-9pm Sun-Tue, to 9:30pm Wed, to 10pm Thu-Sat; 🚌93 from Haymarket, ⛴Inner Harbor Ferry from Long Wharf, 🇹North Station)

Figs   ITALIAN $$

4 🍴 Map p26, B2

This creative pizzeria – which also has an outlet in Beacon Hill – is the brainchild of celebrity chef Todd English, who tops whisper-thin crusts with interesting, exotic toppings. Case in point: the namesake fig and prosciutto with Gorgonzola cheese. The menu also includes sandwiches and fresh pasta. While the food tastes gourmet, the dining room is comfy and casual. (www.toddenglishfigs.com; 67 Main St; mains $16-24; ⏱noon-2:30pm & 5-9:30pm Mon-Fri, noon-10pm Sat, noon-9:30pm Sun; 🖊; 🇹Community College)

Tangierino
MOROCCAN $$$

5 ✖ Map p26, A2

This unexpected gem transports guests from a colonial town house in historic Charlestown to a sultan's palace in the Moroccan desert. North African specialties include *harira* (a traditional tomato and lentil soup), couscous and tagine, all served alongside modern French brasserie fare. The highlight is the sexy interior, complete with thick carpets, plush pillows and rich, jewel-toned tapestries. (📞617-242-6009; www.tangierino.com; 83 Main St; tapas $8-16, mains $19-45; ⏱5-10:30pm Sun-Thu, to 11:30pm Fri & Sat; 🍴; Ⓣ Community College)

Drinking

Warren Tavern
PUB

6 🍺 Map p26, A2

One of the oldest pubs in Boston, the Warren Tavern has been pouring pints for its customers since George Washington and Paul Revere drank here. It is named for General Joseph Warren, a fallen hero of the Battle of Bunker Hill (shortly after which – in 1780 – this pub was opened). Also recommended as a lunch stop (mains $12 to $23). (www.

○ Local Life
Zume's Coffee House

Locals love **Zume's** (Map p26, A1; www.zumescoffeehouse.com; 221 Main St; ⏱6am-4pm Mon-Fri, 7am-4pm Sat & Sun; 📶👶; Ⓣ Community College) – pronounced Zoomie's – for the comfy leather chairs, specialty lattes, decadent doughnuts and homemade English muffins. Also on the menu: soup, sandwiches and lunchy items. Paintings and photographs by local artists adorn the walls; books and tot-sized stools keep the kiddies happy.

warrentavern.com; 2 Pleasant St; ⏱11am-1am Mon-Fri, 10am-1am Sat & Sun; Ⓣ Community College)

Pier Six
BAR

7 🍺 Map p26, E3

Set at the end of the pier behind the Navy Yard, this understated tavern offers one of the loveliest views of the Boston Harbor and city skyline. The food is not that memorable, but it's a fine place to go to catch some rays on your face, the breeze off the water and to enjoy an ice-cold one from behind the bar. (www.pier6boston.com; 1 Eighth St, Pier 6; ⏱11am-1am; 🚌93 from Haymarket, ⛴Inner Harbor Ferry from Long Wharf, Ⓣ North Station)

Explore

West End & North End

Although the West End and North End are physically adjacent, they are atmospherically worlds apart. The West End is an institutional area without much zest. By contrast, the North End is delightfully spicy, thanks to the many Italian *ristoranti* and *salumerie* (delis) that line the streets.

The Sights in a Day

☀ Spend the morning gawking at dinosaur bones, spying on butterflies, programming robots and investigating alternative energy, all at the **Museum of Science** (p36). For lunch, stroll into the North End for pizza from **Galleria Umberto** (p38) or shellfish from **Neptune Oyster** (p37).

☀ Now you are perfectly placed to spend your afternoon exploring the North End. Visit the **Paul Revere House** (p36) at North Sq, then stroll and shop along Hanover St. Traverse the Paul Revere Mall to arrive at **Old North Church** (p36), and continue on to **Copp's Hill Burying Ground** (p36).

🌙 Pick a North End establishment for dinner and treat yourself to an Italian feast. Afterward, have a drink at **Caffè Vittoria** (p40) or catch a show at **Improv Asylum** (p42).

For a local's day in the North End, see p32.

◯ Local Life

Italian Culture in the North End (p32)

❤ Best of Boston

Eating
Pomodoro (p38)

Neptune Oyster (p37)

Galleria Umberto (p38)

Pizzeria Regina (p38)

Drinking
Ward 8 (p40)

Caffè Paradiso (p33)

Caffè dello Sport (p40)

Entertainment
Improv Asylum (p42)

Shopping
Sedurre (p43)

Getting There

🇹 **Metro** Take the green or orange line to Haymarket.

Local Life
Italian Culture in the North End

The North End's warren of alleyways retains the old-world flavor brought by Italian immigrants, ever since they started settling here in the early 20th century. And when we say 'flavor,' we're not being metaphorical. We mean garlic, basil and oregano, sautéed in extra-virgin olive oil; rich tomato sauces that have simmered for hours; amaretto and anise; and crunchy, ricotta-filled cannoli.

....

❶ North End Park
Grab a snack from **Maria's Pastry** (Map p34, F3; www.mariaspastry.com; 46 Cross St; pastries $2-5; ⊙7am-7pm Mon-Sat, to 5pm Sun; ✐; TⓗHaymarket), then cross the street to sit in the shade under grape vines in **North End Park** (www.rosekennedygreenway.org; TⓗHaymarket), designed as the neighborhood's 'front porch.'

❷ Polcari's Coffee

Since 1932, **Polcari's Coffee** (www.
polcariscoffee.com; 105 Salem St; ⏱10am-
6pm Mon-Fri, 9am-6pm Sat; Ⓣ Haymarket)
is where North Enders have stocked
up on their beans. It has 27 kinds of
imported coffee, over 150 spices and
an impressive selection of legumes,
grains and loose teas.

❸ North End Branch Library

The **local library** (www.bpl.org/branches/
north.php; 25 Parmenter St; admission free;
⏱10am-6pm Mon, Tue & Thu, noon-8pm Wed,
9am-5pm Fri, 9am-2pm Sat; Ⓣ Haymarket)
contains an impressive plaster model
of the Palazzo Ducale in Venice, built
in the early 20th century by Henrietta
Macy, a local artist and school teacher
who moved to Venice but never forgot
her Boston students. Figurines of
16th-century Venetians show off the
fashions of the era.

❹ Caffè Paradiso

Stop in at this classic neighborhood
cafe (255 Hanover St; ⏱7am-2am; 📶;
Ⓣ Haymarket) for cappuccino and some
of Boston's finest cannoli (crisp pastry
tubes filled on the spot with creamy
sweetened ricotta cheese). Regulars
watch Italian football on TV while
the bartender masterfully minds the
espresso machine and pours neat
cognacs with understated finesse.

❺ Salumeria Italiana

Salumeria Italiana (www.salumeri-
aitaliana.com; 151 Richmond St; ⏱8am-7pm
Mon-Sat, 10am-4pm Sun; Ⓣ Haymarket) is
the archetype of North End specialty shops, with its shelves stocked
with extra-virgin olive oil and aged
balsamic vinegar, cases crammed with
cured meats, hard cheeses and olives,
boxes of pasta and jars of sauce.

❻ St Leonard's Church

St Leonard's (www.saintleonardchurchbos-
ton.org; 320 Hanover St; ⏱9:30am-2:30pm;
Ⓣ Haymarket), founded in 1873, was the
first church in New England built by
Italian immigrants. If it's open, take a
look inside to see the city's oldest shrine
to St Anthony, most beloved of Italian
saints. The Peace Garden is always
open for a sacred moment of serenity.

❼ All Saints Way

'Mock all and sundry things, but leave
the saints alone' – so goes an old Italian saying posted on the wall of a tiny
alleyway and surrounded by thousands
of images of saints. The **shrine** (4 Battery
St; Ⓣ Haymarket) is the pet project of
Peter Baldassari, a local resident who's
been collecting holy cards since his
childhood here in the 1940s and 1950s.

❽ Langone Park

This peaceful waterside **park** (Commercial St; Ⓣ North Station), designed by
Frederick Law Olmsted, belies the history of this site: in 1919 a huge distill-
ery tank burst, resulting in a flood of
molasses that destroyed homes, killed
21 people and injured hundreds more.
Nowadays, you'll see North Enders
speaking Italian and playing bocce.
Take in the harbor views and enjoy!

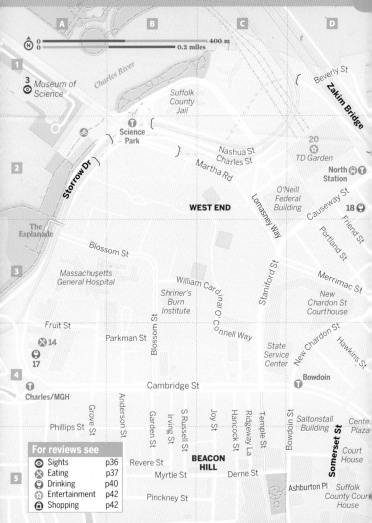

A B C D

1

0 400 m
0 0.2 miles

3 Museum of Science

Charles River

Suffolk County Jail

Science Park

Nashua St
Charles St
Martha Rd

20
TD Garden

North Station

Beverly St

Zakim Bridge

2

Storrow Dr

WEST END

O'Neill Federal Building

Lomasney Way

Causeway St

18

Friend St

Portland St

The Esplanade

Blossom St

Massachusetts General Hospital

Shriner's Burn Institute

William Cardinal O'Connell Way

Staniford St

Merrimac St

New Chardon St Courthouse

3

Fruit St

14

17

Parkman St

Blossom St

State Service Center

New Chardon St

Hawkins St

Bowdoin

4

Charles/MGH

Cambridge St

Phillips St

Grove St

Anderson St

Garden St

Irving St

S Russell St

Joy St

Hancock St

Ridgeway La

Temple St

Bowdoin St

Somerset St

Saltonstall Building

Cente Plaza

Court House

Revere St

BEACON HILL

Myrtle St

Derne St

Ashburton Pl

Suffolk County Cour House

Pinckney St

For reviews see

◎ Sights   p36
✖ Eating   p37
🅟 Drinking   p40
✪ Entertainment   p42
🅐 Shopping   p42

5

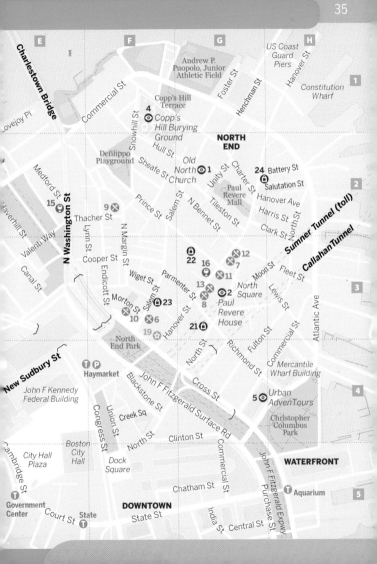

Charlestown Bridge

Lovejoy Pl

Commercial St

E

US Coast
Guard
Piers

Hanover St

Constitution
Wharf

H

1

Andrew P.
Puopolo, Junior
Athletic Field

Foster St

Henchman St

F

G

Copp's Hill
Terrace

Snowhill St

4
◉ Copp's
Hill Burying
Ground

Hull St

Defilippo
Playground

Sheafe St

Old
North
Church

◉ **1**

Unity St

Charter St

**NORTH
END**

24 Battery St

Salutation St

Prince St

Salem St

N Bennet St

Paul
Revere
Mall

Hanover Ave

Harris St

Clark St

North St

Medford St

15
◉

N Washington St

Thacher St

9 ✕

Tileston St

Sumner Tunnel (toll)

2

Haverhill St

Valenti Way

Canal St

Lynn St

Cooper St

N Margin St

Endicott St

Wiget St

Parmenter St

22 🔒

16
♿

✕ **12**
✕ **7**

Moon St

Fleet St

Callahan Tunnel

13
✕ **11**

3

Morton St

Salem St 🔒 **23**

✕ **10** ✕ **6**

Hanover St

8

◉ **2**
Paul
Revere
House

North
Square

Lewis St

Atlantic Ave

19 ✿

North St

21 🔒

Richmond St

Fulton St

Commercial St

John F Kennedy
Federal Building

🚇🅿
Haymarket

North End Park

New Sudbury St

Blackstone St

John F Fitzgerald Surface Rd

Cross St

Mercantile
Wharf Building

5 ◉
Urban
AdvenTours

4

Congress St

Union St

Creek Sq

Clinton St

Commercial St

Christopher
Columbus
Park

Cambridge St

Boston
City Hall

City Hall
Plaza

North St

Dock
Square

Chatham St

WATERFRONT

John F Fitzgerald Expwy

Purchase St

🚇
Government
Center

Court St

State
🚇

DOWNTOWN

State St

India St

Central St

🚇 Aquarium

5

Sights

Old North Church
CHURCH

1 ◉ Map p34, G2

Longfellow's poem *Paul Revere's Ride* has immortalized this graceful church. It was here, on the night of April 18, 1775, that the sexton hung two lanterns from the steeple, as a signal that the British would advance on Lexington and Concord via the sea route. Also called Christ Church, this 1723 Anglican place of worship is Boston's oldest church. (www.oldnorth. com; 193 Salem St; requested donation $3, tour adult/child $6/4; ⊙9am-6pm Jun-Oct, 9am-5pm Mar-May, Nov & Dec, 10am-4pm Jan & Feb; T Haymarket; North Station)

Paul Revere House
HISTORIC SITE

2 ◉ Map p34, G3

When silversmith Paul Revere rode to warn patriots of the British march to Lexington and Concord, he set out from this home on North Sq. This small clapboard house was built in 1680, making it the oldest house in Boston. A self-guided tour through the house and courtyard gives a glimpse of what life was like for the Revere family (which included 16 children!). (www.paulreverehouse.org; 19 North Sq; adult/child $5/1; ⊙9:30am-5:15pm mid-Apr–Oct, to 4:15pm Nov–mid-Apr, closed Mon Jan-Mar; T Haymarket)

Museum of Science
MUSEUM

3 ◉ Map p34, A1

This educational playground has more than 600 interactive exhibits. Favorites include the world's largest lightning-bolt generator, a full-scale space capsule, a world population meter and an impressive dinosaur exhibit. Kids and adults alike can go wild exploring computers and technology, maps and models, the birds and the bees, and human evolution. Recent additions include the Hall of Human Life, where visitors can witness the hatching of baby chicks, and the Yawkey Gallery, with dramatic floor-to-ceiling windows overlooking the Charles River. (www. mos.org; Charles River Dam; adult/child $25/20; ⊙9am-7pm Sat-Thu Jul & Aug, to 5pm Sep-Jun, to 9pm Fri year-round; P ♿; T Science Park/West End)

Copp's Hill Burying Ground
CEMETERY

4 ◉ Map p34, F1

The city's second-oldest cemetery – dating to 1660 – is the final resting place for an estimated 10,000 souls. It is named for William Copp, who originally owned this land. While the oldest graves belong to Copp's children, there are several other noteworthy residents. (Hull St; ⊙8am-5pm; T North Station)

Paul Revere House

Urban AdvenTours
CYCLING

5 Map p34, G4

This outfit was founded by avid cyclists who believe the best views of Boston are from a bicycle. And they're right! The City View Ride provides a great overview of how to get around by bike, including ride-bys of some of Boston's best sites. Other specialty tours include Bikes at Night and the Emerald Necklace tour. Bicycles, helmets and water are all provided. (617-670-0637; www.urbanadventours.com; 103 Atlantic Ave; tours from $40, rentals per 24hr $40-75; 9am-8pm Apr-Sep, shorter hours Oct-Mar; Aquarium)

Eating

Neptune Oyster
SEAFOOD $$$

6 Map p34, F3

Neptune's menu hints at Italian, but you'll also find elements of Mexican, French, Southern and old-fashioned New England. The daily seafood specials and impressive raw bar (featuring several kinds of oysters, plus littlenecks, cherrystones, crabs and mussels) confirm that this is not your traditional North End eatery. (617-742-3474; www.neptuneoyster.com; 63 Salem St; mains $19-39; 11:30am-10pm Sun-Thu, to 11pm Fri & Sat; Haymarket)

> ### Understand
> #### West End Museum
> ------------------------------
>
> The West End – formerly a vibrant ethnic neighborhood – was razed by 'urban renewal' in the 1950s. Now it's dominated by concrete monoliths and institutional buildings. The **West End Museum** (www.thewestendmuseum.org; 150 Staniford St; admission free; ☺noon-5pm Tue-Fri, 11am-4pm Sat; ⓣNorth Station) is dedicated to preserving the memory of this neighborhood and educating the public about the ramifications of unchecked urban development. The Last Tenement exhibit traces the history of the neighborhood from 1850 to 1958, highlighting its immigrant populations, economic evolution and eventual destruction.

Pomodoro   ITALIAN $$

| 7 🍴 | Map p34, G3 |

Seductive Pomodoro offers one of the North End's most romantic settings for delectable Italian. The food is simple but perfectly prepared: fresh pasta, spicy tomato sauce, grilled fish and meats, and wine by the glass. If you're lucky, you might be on the receiving end of a complimentary tiramisu for dessert. Cash only. (☎617-367-4348; 351 Hanover St; mains $23-24; ☺5:30-11pm; ⓣHaymarket)

Galleria Umberto   PIZZA $

| 8 🍴 | Map p34, G3 |

Paper plates, cans of soda, Sicilian pizza: can't beat it. This lunchtime legend closes as soon as the slices are gone. And considering their thick and chewy goodness, that's often before the official 2:30pm closing time. Loyal patrons line up early so they are sure to get theirs. Other snacking options include calzone, panini and arancini. Cash only. (289 Hanover St; mains $2-5; ☺10:45am-2:30pm Mon-Sat; ✈; ⓣHaymarket)

Pizzeria Regina   PIZZA $

| 9 🍴 | Map p34, F2 |

The queen of North End pizzerias is the legendary Pizzeria Regina, famous for brusque but endearing waitstaff and crispy, thin-crust pizza. Thanks to the slightly spicy sauce (flavored with aged Romano), Regina repeatedly wins accolades for its pies. Reservations are not accepted, so be prepared to wait. (www.pizzeriaregina.com; 11½ Thacher St; pizzas $13-21; ☺11am-11:30pm Sun-Thu, to 12:30am Fri & Sat; ✈; ⓣHaymarket)

Maria's Pastry   BAKERY $

| 10 🍴 | Map p34, F3 |

Three generations of Merola women are now working to bring you Boston's most authentic Italian pastries.

Many claim that Maria makes the best cannoli in the North End, but you'll also find more elaborate concoctions like *sfogliatelle* (layered, shell-shaped pastry filled with ricotta) and *aragosta* (cream-filled 'lobster tail' pastry). Note the early closing time: eat dessert first! (www.mariaspastry.com; 46 Cross St; pastries $2-5; ⏰7am-7pm Mon-Sat, to 5pm Sun; 🖊; Ⓣ Haymarket)

Daily Catch   SEAFOOD $$

11 🍴 Map p34, G3

Although owner Paul Freddura long ago added a few tables and an open kitchen, this shoebox fish joint still retains the atmosphere of a retail fish market (complete with wine served in plastic cups). Fortunately, it also retains the freshness of the fish. The specialty is *tinta de calamari* (squid-ink pasta). Cash only. (http://thedailycatch.com; 323 Hanover St; mains lunch $10-18, dinner $20-29; ⏰11am-10pm; Ⓣ Haymarket)

Giacomo's Ristorante   ITALIAN $$

12 🍴 Map p34, G3

Customers line up before the doors open so they can guarantee themselves a spot in the first round of seating at this North End favorite. Enthusiastic and entertaining waitstaff plus cramped quarters ensure that you get to know your neighbors. The cuisine is no-frills southern Italian fare, served in unbelievable portions. Cash only. (www.giacomosblog-boston.blogspot.com; 355 Hanover St; mains $15-20; ⏰4:30-10pm Mon-Thu, to 10:30pm Fri & Sat, 4-9:30pm Sun; 🖊; Ⓣ Haymarket)

Carmelina's   ITALIAN $$

13 🍴 Map p34, G3

There's a lot to look at when you sit down at Carmelina's, whether you face the busy, open kitchen or the massive windows overlooking Hanover St. This understated, contemporary space serves up Sicilian dishes with a modern American twist – customers are crazy about the Crazy Alfredo and the Sunday Macaroni (which is served every day, in case you're wondering). (www.carmelinasboston.com; 307 Hanover St; mains $16-29; ⏰noon-10pm; 🖊; Ⓣ Haymarket)

Scampo   ITALIAN $$$

14 🍴 Map p34, A4

Celeb chef Lydia Shire is the brains and brawn behind this trendy restaurant on the ground floor of the Liberty Hotel. Buzzing with energy, Scampo offers handmade pasta and irresistible thin-crust pizza, as well as a full mozzarella bar. The extensive gluten-free menu is a bonus. (📞617-536-2100; www.scampoboston.com; 215 Charles St; mains lunch $14-28, dinner $18-48; ⏰11:30am-2:30pm & 5:30-10pm Sun-Wed, to 11pm Thu-Sat; 🖊; Ⓣ Charles/MGH)

Drinking

Ward 8   COCKTAIL BAR

15 [T] Map p34, E2

The bartenders at this throwback know their stuff, mixing up a slew of specialty cocktails (including the namesake Ward 8) and serving them in clever thematic containers. The menu also features craft beers and tempting New American cuisine (try the maple chili duck wings). The atmosphere is classy but convivial – an excellent addition to the North End–West End scene. (www.ward8. com; 90 N Washington St; ⏰11:30am-1am Mon-Wed, to 11:30am-2am Thu & Fri, 10am-2am Sat, 10am-1am Sun; [T]North Station; Haymarket)

Caffè Vittoria   CAFE

16 [T] Map p34, G3

A delightful destination for dessert or aperitifs, this frilly parlor displays antique espresso machines and black-and-white photos, with a pressed-tin ceiling reminiscent of the Victorian era. Grab a marble-topped table, order a cappuccino and enjoy the romantic setting. Cash only, just like the olden days. (www.caffevittoria.com; 290-296 Hanover St; ⏰7am-midnight; 📶; [T]Haymarket)

Alibi   COCKTAIL BAR

17 [T] Map p34, A4

Housed in the former Charles St Jail, this hot-to-trot drinking venue is set in the old 'drunk tank' (holding cell for the intoxicated). The prison theme is played up, with mugshots hanging on the brick walls and iron bars on the doors and windows. Prices are high and service can be lacking, but it's fun to drink in jail. Dress sharp. (www.alibiboston.com; 215 Charles St, Liberty Hotel; ⏰5pm-2am; [T]Charles/MGH)

Boston Beer Works   BREWERY

18 [T] Map p34, D2

Boston Beer Works is a solid option for beer lovers and sports lovers (conveniently located near the city's major sporting venues). The excellent selection of microbrews offers something for everyone, including plenty of seasonal specialties. Fruity brews like blueberry ale get rave reviews, with tasty sour-cream-chive fries as the perfect accompaniment. (www.beerworks. net; 112 Canal St; ⏰11am-11pm Sun-Thu, to 1am Fri & Sat; [T]North Station)

◯ Local Life
Drinking in the North End
Watch football, drink Campari and speak Italian (or just listen) at **Caffè dello Sport** (Map p34, G3; www.caffedellosport.us; 308 Hanover St; ⏰6am-midnight Mon-Fri, from 7am Sat & Sun; 📶; [T]Haymarket) or Caffè Paradiso (p33).

Understand

Revolutionary Boston

Called the Birthplace of the American Revolution, Boston played an incendiary role in the colonies' fight for independence.

No Taxation Without Representation

In the 1760s the British Parliament passed a series of acts that placed greater financial burdens on the colonists. With each new tax, resentment in Boston intensified, as did vocal protests and violent mobs. Respected lawyer John Adams cited the Magna Carta's principle of 'no taxation without representation.' To each act of rebellion, the British throne responded with increasingly severe measures, eventually dispatching Redcoats to restore order and suspending all local political power in Boston.

Sons of Liberty

Unrepentant Bostonians went underground. The Sons of Liberty, a clandestine network of patriots, led resistance to British policy and harassed the king's loyalists. Led by some well-known townsmen – including surgeon Dr Joseph Warren, merchant John Hancock, silversmith Paul Revere and brewer Sam Adams – they organized protests, instigating the Boston Massacre (p48) and advocating for the Boston Tea Party (p67).

After the Tea Party, the port was blockaded and Boston placed under military rule. The Sons of Liberty spread news of this latest outrage down the seaboard. The cause of Boston was becoming the cause of all the colonies – American independence versus British tyranny.

The Shot Heard Round the World

In April 1775 British General Gage dispatched troops to arrest fugitives Sam Adams and John Hancock and to seize a cache of gunpowder. Informants tipped off Joseph Warren, who told the Old North Church sexton to hang two lanterns in the steeple – a signal to Paul Revere, who galloped on his horse through the night to alert the local militia, the Minutemen.

At daybreak, the confrontation occurred. British troops skirmished with Minutemen on the Old North Bridge in Concord and on the Lexington Green. By midmorning, more militia had arrived and chased the Redcoats back to Boston in ignominious defeat. The inevitable had arrived: the War for Independence.

Ward 8

Back in the day, Ward 8 was the political division that encompassed the West End – the territory of local politician and 'ward boss' Martin Lomasney. Also known as 'the Mahatma,' Lomasney was a key player in the Democratic Party machine, adept at trading in political favors and patronage.

His long political legacy includes the quintessential Boston cocktail, the Ward 8. As the story goes, Lomasney gathered with his supporters on the eve of his election to the state legislature. His victory was a foregone conclusion, so the bartender at the venerable Locke-Ober Restaurant created a new drink to celebrate. The resulting cocktail, essentially a whiskey sour with a dash of grenadine, was named for the district that would swing the election.

Ironically, Lomasney was a Prohibitionist, and after his election this cocktail and others were outlawed. That's not doing anyone any favors, Mr Lomasney.

Entertainment

Improv Asylum   COMEDY

19 ⭐ Map p34, F3

A basement theater is somehow the perfect setting for the dark humor spewing from the mouths of this off-beat crew. No topic is too touchy, no politics too correct. Shows vary from night to night, but the standard Main-stage Show mixes up the improv with comedy sketches that are guaranteed to make you giggle. (www.improvasylum. com; 216 Hanover St; tickets $7-28; ⏰shows 8pm Sun-Thu, 7:30pm, 10pm & midnight Fri & Sat; Ⓣ Haymarket)

TD Garden   STADIUM

20 ⭐ Map p34, D2

The TD Garden is home to the NHL Boston Bruins, who play hockey here from September to June, and the NBA Boston Celtics, who play basketball from October to April. It's the city's largest venue, so big-name musicians perform here, too. (📞event info 617-624-1000; www.tdgarden.com; 150 Causeway St; Ⓣ North Station)

Shopping

North Bennet Street School

ARTS & CRAFTS

21 🔒 Map p34, G3

The North Bennet Street School has been training craftspeople for over 100 years. Established in 1885, the school offers programs in traditional skills like bookbinding, woodworking and locksmithing. The school's on-site gallery sells incredible hand-crafted pieces made by students and alumni. Look for unique jewelry, handmade journals, and exquisite wooden furniture and musical instruments. (www.nbss.edu/shopnbss-store; 150 North St; ☉9am-3pm Mon-Fri; ⊤Haymarket)

Sedurre CLOTHING

22 🔒 Map p34, G3

If you speak Italian, you'll know that Sedurre's thing is sexy and stylish. (It means 'seduce.') The shop started with fine lingerie – beautiful lacy nightgowns and underthings for special occasions. Sisters Robyn and Daria were so good at that, they created an additional space next door for dresses, evening wear and jewelry (for other kinds of special occasions). (www.sedurreboston.com; 28½ Prince St; ☉11am-7pm Mon-Wed, to 8pm Thu & Fri, to 9pm Sat, noon-6pm Sun; ⊤Haymarket)

Shake the Tree FASHION & ACCESSORIES

23 🔒 Map p34, F3

You never know what you will find at this sweet boutique, but it's bound to be good. This little shop carries a wonderful, eclectic assortment of jewelry by local artisans, alongside interesting stationery, designer handbags and clothing, and unique housewares. (www.shakethetreeboston.com; 67 Salem St; ☉11am-7pm Mon-Fri, 10am-8pm Sat, noon-5pm Sun; ⊤Haymarket)

In-Jean-ius CLOTHING

24 🔒 Map p34, G2

You know what you're getting when you waltz into this denim haven. Offerings from more than 20 designers include tried-and-true favorites and little-known gems, and staff are on hand to help you find the perfect pair. Warning: the surgeon general has determined that it is not healthy to try on jeans after a gigantic plate of pasta; come here before dinner. (www.injeanius.com; 441 Hanover St; ☉11am-7pm Mon-Sat, noon-6pm Sun; ⊤Haymarket)

Explore

Beacon Hill & Boston Common

Abutted by the Boston Common – the nation's original public park and the centerpiece of the city – and topped with the gold-domed Massachusetts State House, Beacon Hill is the neighborhood most often featured on Boston postcards. The retail and residential streets on Beacon Hill are delightfully, quintessentially Boston.

The Sights in a Day

☀ Start your day with breakfast at the **Paramount** (p53) or coffee and pastries at **Tatte** (p53). Then dedicate your morning to exploring the first few sites along the Freedom Trail, starting at the **Boston Common** (p46), touring the **Massachusetts State House** (p52) and investigating the ancient headstones in the **Granary Burying Ground** (p52).

☀ If the weather is fine, enjoy a picnic lunch in the **Public Garden** (p52). Your afternoon is free for browsing the boutiques and shopping for antiques along Charles St. Take a detour to marvel at the architecture on **Louisburg Square** (p135) and check out the current exhibit at the **Museum of African American History** (p53).

☾ When it's time for a break, beer-lovers should head to **Tip Tap Room** (p54) to sample from 40 kinds of craft beer, while wine drinkers might prefer **Bin 26 Enoteca** (p54). Stay for dinner or venture to one of Beacon Hill's other fine eating establishments.

Top Sights
◉ Boston Common (p46)

♥ Best of Boston

Eating
Tatte (p53)

Drinking
21st Amendment (p54)

Tip Tap Room (p54)

Shopping
Crush Boutique (p55)

Getting There

Ⓣ **Metro** Take the green or red lines to Park St.

Top Sights
Boston Common

The 50-acre Boston Common is the country's oldest public park. The Common has served many purposes over the years, including as a campground for British troops during the Revolutionary War and as green grass for cattle grazing until the 1830s. Although there is still a grazing ordinance on the books, the Common today serves picnickers, sunbathers and people-watchers.

◉ Map p50, E4

btwn Tremont, Charles, Beacon & Park Sts

🕑 6am–midnight

P 🚼

T Park St

Parkman Bandstand, Boston Common

Blaxton Plaque
The Reverend William Blaxton was the first European settler of Boston. In 1634 he sold this land to the Massachusetts Bay Colony for £30. A plaque emblazoned with the words of the treaty between Governor Winthrop and Reverend Blaxton is located at the corner of Park and Tremont Sts.

Brewer Fountain
This bronze beauty dates to 1868, when it was gifted to the city of Boston by wealthy merchant Gardner Brewer. The fountain features four aquatic deities from antiquity: the Roman god of water, Neptune; the Greek sea goddess, Amphitrite; and the spirit Acis and sea nymph Galatea, both from Ovid's *Metamorphoses*. The design won a gold medal at the 1855 World's Fair.

Robert Gould Shaw Memorial
Sculpted by Augustus St Gaudens, this magnificent bas-relief memorial opposite the State House honors the 54th Massachusetts Regiment of the Union Army, the nation's first all-black Civil War regiment (depicted in the 1989 film *Glory*). Shaw – the son of a wealthy Brahmin family – and half his men were killed in a battle at Fort Wagner, South Carolina.

Soldiers & Sailors Monument
Dedicated in 1877, this massive monument atop Flagstaff Hill pays tribute to the namesake soldiers and sailors who died in the Civil War. The four bronze statues represent Peace (facing south); the Sailor (facing the ocean); History (looking to heaven); and the Soldier (standing at ease). Many historical figures are cast in the elaborate bronze reliefs.

☑ Top Tips
▶ The Boston Common is often called 'the Common' in local parlance, but never 'the Commons.' Use the singular or risk ridicule by locals!

▶ The on-site information kiosk is a great source of information, maps etc.

▶ The kiosk is also the starting place for guided tours by the Freedom Trail Foundation.

✗ Take a Break
Various food trucks park near the entrance to the Park St T station. Our favorite is Clover Food Lab (www.cloverfoodlab.com).

Alternatively, check out the **Earl of Sandwich** (www.earlofsandwichusa.com; 1b Charles St, Boston Common; sandwiches $5.50-8; ⏱11am-6pm daily May-Oct, 11am-4pm Mon-Fri Nov-Apr; T Park St, Boylston), located in the handsome 'Pink Palace'.

Understand
The Boston Massacre

In front of the Old State House, encircled by cobblestones, a bronze plaque marks the spot where the first blood was shed for the American independence movement.

On March 5, 1770, an angry mob of colonists swarmed the British soldiers guarding the State House. Sam Adams, John Hancock and about 40 other protesters hurled snowballs, rocks and insults. Thus provoked, the soldiers fired into the crowd and killed five townspeople, including Crispus Attucks, a former slave.

The incident sparked enormous anti-British sentiment. Paul Revere helped fan the flames by widely disseminating an engraving that depicted the scene as an unmitigated slaughter. Interestingly, John Adams and Josiah Quincy – both of whom opposed the heavy-handed authoritarian British rule – defended the accused soldiers in court, and seven of the nine were acquitted.

Boston Massacre Monument

This 25ft monument pays tribute to the five victims of the Boston Massacre, which took place down the street near the Old State House. It replicates Paul Revere's famous engraving of this tragic event. Revere's effective propaganda depicts the soldiers shooting down defenseless colonists in cold blood, when in reality they were reacting to the aggressive crowd in self-defense.

Great Elm Site

A plaque marks the site of the **Old Elm** that stood here for more than 200 years. History has it that accused witches were hanged here, and the Sons of Liberty (a clandestine network of patriots) hung lanterns on its branches as a symbol of unity.

Boston's 'oldest inhabitant' was destroyed by a storm in 1876.

Frog Pond

When temperatures drop, the Boston Common becomes an urban winter wonderland, with slipping and sliding, swirling and twirling on the **Frog Pond** (www.bostonfrogpond.com; adult/child $6/free, rental $12/6; ☉10am-3:45pm Mon, to 9pm Tue-Thu & Sun, to 10pm Fri & Sat mid-Nov–mid-Mar). In summer it's a spray pool where tiny tots can cool off.

Central Burying Ground

Dating to 1756, the **Central Burying Ground** (Boylston St; ☉9am-5pm; T Boylston) is the least celebrated of the old cemeteries, as it was the burial ground of the down-and-out – according to an account in

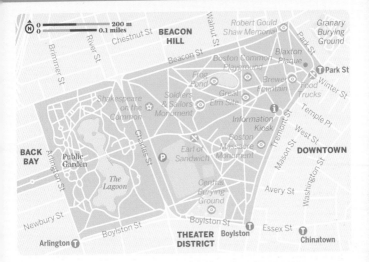

Edwin Bacon's *Boston Illustrated*, it was used for 'Roman Catholics and strangers dying in the town.' The most recognized name here is that of noted portrait artist Gilbert Stuart.

Tadpole Playground

We're not sure if America's first public park is also home to its first playground, but rest assured, this one has a huge playscape with swings, jungle gyms and a carousel.

Shakespeare on the Common

Each summer, the Commonwealth Shakespeare Company stages a major production on the Boston Common, drawing crowds for theater under the stars. **Productions** (www.commshakes.org; ⊙ Jul & Aug) often appeal to the masses with a populist twist, such as *The Taming of the Shrew* set in a North End restaurant.

Charles/MGH 🚇

Phillips St

Grove St

Anderson St

🔒 11

Revere St

Pinckney St 🔒
10

Louisburg
Square

5 🍴 Charles St

W Cedar St

Cedar La Way

12 🔒

🍴 6

Acorn St

Willow St

Lime St

River St

Chestnut St

Branch St

Hatch
Memorial
Shell

Embankment Rd

The
Esplanade

Brimmer St

Byron St

9 🚻

Charles River

Charles River Bike Path

Charles River

Storrow Dr

Back St

1 🎯
Public
Garden

Beacon St

**BACK
BAY**

Marlborough St

Berkeley St

Arlington St

Charles St

P

Clarendon St

Commonwealth Ave Mall

Ritz
Carlton
Hotel

The
Lagoon

Commonwealth Ave

Newbury St

Ⓝ 0
0   400 m
         0.2 miles

🚇 Arlington

Boylston St

E

WEST END

Cambridge St

F

🚇 Bowdoin

G

Cambridge St

H

1

City Hall Plaza

Boston City Hall

Garden St

Irving St

S Russell St

Joy St

Hancock St

Temple St

Ridgeway La

8

Bowdoin St

Center Plaza

Court House

Smith Ct

4 ◉

Museum of African American History

Suffolk University

Derne St

Ashburton Pl

Somerset St

Government Center 🚇

Court St

Court Sq

State 🚇

2

Myrtle St

BEACON HILL

Mt Vernon St

Joy St

◉

Massachusetts State House

Ashburton Park

Tremont St

School St

Court St

Washington St

2

Walnut St

7 ◉

Granary Burying Ground

◉ **3**

Bosworth St

Province St

Milk St

Beacon St

Park St

Bromfield St

DOWNTOWN

Hawley St

Arch St

3

Park St 🚇

Boston Common Information Kiosk ℹ️

Cathedral Church of St Paul

Winter St

Downtown 🚇 Crossing

Franklin St

Snow Pl

Boston Common ◉

Tremont St

Temple Pl

West St

Mason St

Washington St

Macy's

Chauncy St

Otis St

4

Opera House

Avery St

Millennium Place

Ave de Lafayette

Harrison Ave Ext

Central Burying Ground

Boylston St

Boylston 🚇

Essex St

Chinatown 🚇

For reviews see	
◉ Top Sights	p46
◉ Sights	p52
✕ Eating	p53
🍷 Drinking	p54
🛍 Shopping	p54

5

DIEGO GRANDI/SHUTTERSTOCK ©

Paul Revere's grave, Granary Burying Ground

Sights

Public Garden
GARDENS

1  Map p50, C4

Adjoining Boston Common, the Public Garden is a 24-acre botanical oasis of Victorian flower beds, verdant grass and weeping willow trees shading a tranquil lagoon. The old-fashioned pedal-powered **Swan Boats** (www.swanboats.com; adult/child $3.50/2; ⏱10am-4pm mid-Apr–mid-Jun, to 5pm late Jun-Aug, noon-4pm 1st half of Sep; T Arlington) have been delighting children for generations. The most endearing spot in the Public Garden is the **Make Way for Ducklings Statue**, depicting the main characters in the beloved book by Robert McCloskey.

(www.friendsofthepublicgarden.org; Arlington St; ⏱dawn-dusk; ♿; T Arlington)

Massachusetts State House
NOTABLE BUILDING

2  Map p50, F2

High atop Beacon Hill, Massachusetts' leaders and legislators attempt to turn their ideas into concrete policies and practices within the State House. John Hancock provided the land (previously part of his cow pasture); Charles Bulfinch designed the commanding state capitol; but it was Oliver Wendell Holmes who called it 'the hub of the solar system' (thus earning Boston the nickname 'the Hub'). Free 40-minute tours cover the history, artwork, architecture and political personalities of the State House. (www.sec.state.ma.us; cnr Beacon & Bowdoin Sts; admission free; ⏱8:45am-5pm Mon-Fri, tours 10am-3:30pm Mon-Fri; T Park St)

Granary Burying Ground
CEMETERY

3  Map p50, G3

Dating to 1660, this atmospheric atoll is crammed with historic headstones, many with evocative (and creepy) carvings. This is the final resting place of all your favorite revolutionary heroes, including Paul Revere, Samuel Adams, John Hancock and James Otis. Benjamin Franklin is buried in Philadelphia, but the Franklin family plot contains his parents. (Tremont St; ⏱9am-5pm; T Park St)

Museum of African American History   MUSEUM

4 ⊙ Map p50, E1

The Museum of African American History occupies two adjacent historic buildings: the African Meeting House, the country's oldest black church and meeting house; and Abiel Smith School, the country's first school for blacks. The museum offers rotating exhibits about the historic events that took place here, and is also a source of information about – and the final destination of – the **Black Heritage Trail** (www.nps.gov/boaf; ⊙tours 10am, noon & 1pm Mon-Sat Jul & Aug; T Park St). This 1.6-mile trail explores the history of the abolitionist movement and African American settlement on Beacon Hill. The National Park Service (NPS) conducts guided tours, but maps and descriptions for self-guided tours are available at the Museum of African American History. (www.maah. org; 46 Joy St; adult/child $5/free; ⊙10am-4pm Mon-Sat; T Park St, Bowdoin)

Eating

Tatte   BAKERY $

5 ✗ Map p50, C2

The aroma of buttery goodness – and the lines stretching out the door – signal your arrival at this fabulous bakery on the lower floor of the historic Charles St Meeting House. Swoon-worthy pastries (divinely cinnamon-y morning buns, chocolate-hazelnut twists, avocado and mushroom tartines) taste even more amazing if you're lucky enough to score a table on the sunny front patio. (www.tattebakery.com; 70 Charles St; pastries from $3; ⊙7am-8pm Mon-Fri, 8am-8pm Sat, 8am-7pm Sun; T Charles/MGH)

Paramount   CAFETERIA $$

6 ✗ Map p50, C3

This old-fashioned cafeteria is a neighborhood favorite. A-plus diner fare includes pancakes, home fries, burgers and sandwiches, and big, hearty salads. Banana and caramel French toast is an obvious go-to for the brunch crowd. Don't sit down until you get your food! The wait may seem endless, but patrons swear it is worth it. (www.paramountboston.com; 44 Charles St; mains breakfast & lunch $8-15, dinner $17-24; ⊙7am-10pm Mon-Fri, 8am-10pm Sat & Sun; ✗♿; T Charles/MGH)

Local Life
Hidden Beacon Hill

Take a detour away from Charles St to discover a few Beacon Hill gems. There is no more prestigious address than Louisburg Square (p135), a cluster of stately brick row houses facing a private park. Nearby **Acorn Street** (T Charles/MGH) is Boston's oft-photographed narrowest street. This cobblestone alleyway was once home to artisans and to the service people who worked for the adjacent mansion dwellers.

No 9 Park

EUROPEAN $$$

7 ✕ Map p50, F3

This swanky place has been around for years, but it still tops many fine-dining lists. Chef-owner Barbara Lynch has been lauded by food and wine magazines for her delectable French and Italian culinary master-pieces and her first-rate wine list. She has now cast her celebrity-chef spell all around town, but this is the place that made her famous. Reservations recommended. (☏617-742-9991; www.no9park.com; 9 Park St; mains $37-47, 6-course tasting menu $125; ☉5-9pm Mon-Wed, 5-10pm Thu-Sat, 4-8pm Sun; Ⓣ Park St)

Drinking

Tip Tap Room

BAR

8 🅿 Map p50, F1

The 'tips' are steak, lamb, turkey, chicken or swordfish. The 'taps' are nearly 40 kinds of beer, ranging from local craft brews to international ales of some renown. The food is good (including a daily 'game special' such as braised antelope ribs), and the beer is even better. There's no other place on Beacon Hill with this trendy but friendly vibe. (www.thetiptaproom.com; 138 Cambridge St; ☉11:30am-2am Mon-Fri, 10:30am-2am Sat & Sun; 🛜; Ⓣ Bowdoin)

Bin 26 Enoteca

WINE BAR

9 🅿 Map p50, C3

If you're into your wine, you'll be into the Bin. Big windows overlook

Charles St and wine bottles line the walls. The extensive wine list spans the globe, including a moderately priced house wine that is bottled in Italy just for the restaurant. Staff will insist you order food (due to licensing requirements), but you won't regret sampling the simple, seasonal menu. (☏617-723-5939; www.bin26.com; 26 Charles St; ☉noon-10pm Mon-Fri, 10am-10pm Sat & Sun; Ⓣ Charles/MGH, Arlington)

Shopping

Beacon Hill Chocolates

FOOD & DRINKS

10 🔒 Map p50, C2

This artisanal chocolatier puts equal effort into selecting fine chocolates from around the world and designing beautiful keepsake boxes to contain them. Using decoupage to affix old postcards, photos and illustrations, the boxes are works of art even be-fore they are filled with truffles. Pick

Antiquing on Beacon Hill

There was a time when Charles St was lined with antique shops and nothing else: some historians claim that the country's antique trade began right here on Beacon Hill. Many vestiges remain from those days of yesteryear. Here are a few of our favorites:

Eugene Galleries (www.eugenegalleries.com; 76 Charles St; ⊙11am-6pm Mon-Sat, noon-6pm Sun; ⊤Charles/MGH) A tiny shop with a remarkable selection of antique prints and maps, especially focusing on old Boston.

Marika's Antique Shop (130 Charles St; ⊙11am-6pm Tue-Sat; ⊤Charles/MGH) A treasure trove of jewelry, silver and porcelain.

Twentieth Century Ltd (www.boston-vintagejewelry.com; 73 Charles St; ⊙11am-6pm Mon-Sat, noon-5pm Sun; ⊤Charles/MGH) Vintage costume jewelry, made by the great designers of yesteryear.

out an image of historic Boston as a souvenir for the sweet tooth in your life. (www.beaconhillchocolates.com; 91 Charles St; ⊙11am-7pm Mon-Sat, to 5:30pm Sun; ⊤Charles/MGH)

Crush Boutique   CLOTHING

11 🔒 Map p50, C1

Fashion mavens rave about this cozy basement boutique on Charles St, which features both well-loved designers and up-and-coming talents. The selection of clothing is excellent, but it's the expert advice that makes this place so popular. Co-owners (and childhood BFFs) Rebecca and Laura would love to help you find something that makes you look fabulous. (www.shopcrushboutique.com; 131 Charles

St; ⊙10am-7pm Mon-Sat, 11am-6pm Sun; ⊤Charles/MGH)

Blackstone's of Beacon Hill   GIFTS & SOUVENIRS

12 🔒 Map p50, C3

Here's a guarantee: you will find the perfect gift for that certain someone at Blackstone's. This little place is crammed with classy, clever and otherwise-unusual items. Highlights include the custom-designed stationery, locally made handicrafts, and quirky Boston-themed souvenirs like *Make Way for Ducklings* onesies. Otherwise, you can't go wrong with a solar-powered rotating globe – everyone needs one! (www.blackstonesbeaconhill.com; 46 Charles St; ⊙10am-6:30pm Mon-Fri, to 6pm Sat, 11am-5pm Sun; ⊤Charles/MGH)

Explore

Downtown & the Waterfront

Much of Boston's business and tourist activity takes place in this central neighborhood. Downtown is crammed with historic sites, colonial buildings and modern skyscapers, while across the Fort Point Channel, the Seaport District is fast developing as a waterside destination, thanks to its dynamic contemporary-art museum and an explosion of new dining options.

The Sights in a Day

☀ The Freedom Trail cuts right through downtown Boston. You can spend your morning seeing some of the city's most important historic sites, including the **Old South Meeting House** (p64), **Old State House** (p64) and **Faneuil Hall** (p65). By lunchtime, you're right in the vicinity of **Quincy Market** (p68).

☀ After lunch, stroll across the **Rose Kennedy Greenway** (p65) to reach the waterfront. If you're up for more history, head to the **Boston Tea Party Ships & Museum** (p64). Alternatively, for a change of pace, visit the sea creatures at the **New England Aquarium** (p58) or peruse the diverse creations at the **Institute of Contemporary Art** (p60).

☾ You're in the right place for dinner, as the Seaport District is home to some of Boston's hottest restaurants. Go to **Legal Harborside** (p67) for the view or **Row 34** (p66) for the scene. Finish the night with something delicious created by the mixologists at **Drink** (p68).

👁 Top Sights

New England Aquarium (p58)

Institute of Contemporary Art (p60)

💜 Best of Boston

Eating

Row 34 (p66)

Yankee Lobster Co (p67)

Drinking

Drink (p68)

Highball Lounge (p68)

Harpoon Brewery (p70)

Thinking Cup (p70)

Getting There

T Metro All of the T lines traverse this central neighborhood, with useful stops at Aquarium, Haymarket (for Faneuil Hall), State (the State House) and South Station (the Seaport District).

🚌 Bus SL1 and SL2 silver line buses run from South Station into the Seaport District.

⚓ Boat The MBTA's Inner Harbor Ferry and Boston Harbor Cruises' Water Taxi stop at Long Wharf on the waterfront.

Top Sights
New England Aquarium

Teeming with sea creatures of all sizes, shapes and colors, this giant fishbowl is the centerpiece of downtown Boston's waterfront. The main attraction is the three-story Giant Ocean Tank, which swirls with thousands of creatures great and small, including turtles, sharks and eels. Countless side exhibits explore the lives and habitats of other underwater oddities, as well as penguins and sea mammals.

Map p62, E2

www.neaq.org

Central Wharf

adult/child $27/19

9am-5pm Mon-Fri, to 6pm Sat & Sun, 1hr later Jul & Aug

P T Aquarium

Shark & Ray Touch Tank

The awesome Shark & Ray Touch Tank re-creates a mangrove swamp full of Atlantic rays, cownose rays and five species of shark.

Penguins

Most of the aquarium's 1st floor is occupied by an enormous penguin exhibit, home to three different species and more than 90 birds. Throughout the day, visitors can see live demonstrations and feedings.

Marine Mammals

Harbor seals frolic in a large observation tank near the aquarium entrance, while the open-air Marine Mammal Center out back is home to northern fur seals and California sea lions. Informative training demonstrations are scheduled throughout the day, though all three groups of pinnipeds put on an entertaining show anyway. Note that some animal rights groups make a strong case that marine mammals should not be kept in captivity, no matter how classy their quarters.

Amazon Rainforest

Six different tanks showcase the flora and fauna of the Amazon Rainforest, including piranhas, anacondas, electric eels and poison dart frogs. The exhibits also emphasize the importance of sustainable fishing practices.

☑ **Top Tips**

▶ Buy timed tickets in advance to skip the lines (the 9am slot is best for avoiding crowds).

▶ The 3D **Simons IMAX Theatre** (www. neaq.org; Central Wharf; adult/child $10/8; ⊘first/last screening 10am/6pm Mon-Fri, 10am/7pm Sat & Sun) features films with aquatic themes.

▶ The aquarium also organizes whale-watching cruises (p66). Combination tickets are available.

✖ **Take a Break**

There are several options for lunch on Aquarium Plaza, including the **Reef** (www.neaq. org; Aquarium Plaza; mains $10-16; ⊘11am-8pm daily Jun-Aug, 11am-6pm Thu-Sun May, Sep & Oct; 🖋), a seasonal outdoor restaurant serving lobster rolls, clam chowder and steamers, with a side of sea breezes.

Top Sights
Institute of Contemporary Art

Boston is becoming a focal point for contemporary art in the 21st century, as hundreds of thousands of visitors flock to the dramatic quarters of the Institute of Contemporary Art – the building is a work of art in itself. The spacious light-filled interior hosts multimedia presentations, educational programs and studio space. More importantly, it's the venue for the development of the ICA's permanent collection of 21st-century art.

Map p62, F3

www.icaboston.org

25 Harbor Shore Dr

adult/child $15/free

10am-5pm Tue, Wed, Sat & Sun, to 9pm Thu & Fri

SL1, SL2, South Station

Founders Gallery

Arguably, the ICA building and setting are as much of an attraction as the art. Opened in 2006, the structure skillfully incorporates its surroundings into the architecture. In the Founders Gallery, which spans the entire width of the building, a glass wall virtually eliminates any barrier between viewer and seascape.

Permanent Collection

In addition to dynamic temporary exhibits, the ICA showcases national and international artists in its permanent collection. You'll find the likes of graffiti artist Shepard Fairey, conceptual artist Gillian Wearing, video artist Christian Jankowski, photographer Boris Mikhailov and sculptor Sarah Sze. Look for all manner of art, from painting to video to multidimensional mixed-media mash-ups.

Mediatheque

The Mediatheque is the museum's digital media center, where visitors can use the computer stations to learn more about featured art and artists. The terraced room has a wall of windows at the front, but the room's unique downward-slanting perspective shows only the dancing and rippling of water, with no horizon in sight.

Barbara Lee Family Foundation Theater

The Barbara Lee Family Foundation Theater is one of the ICA's coolest features. With a wooden floor and ceiling and glass walls, the two-story venue is an extension of the boardwalk outside. It's a remarkable backdrop for edgy theater, dance, music and other performance art.

☑ Top Tips

▶ Take advantage of the ICA audio commentary that is available free with admission. Borrow an iPod from the front desk or download the tracks to your own device from the museum's website.

▶ The ICA offers guided thematic tours on Saturday and Sunday (1pm and 2:30pm) and Thursday evenings (6pm and 7pm).

▶ Admission is free for all on Thursdays after 5pm.

▶ Admission is always free for kids aged 17 and under.

✗ Take a Break

On the ICA's ground floor, the **Water Cafe** (mains $8-11; ⊘11am to 4pm Tue, Wed, Sat, Sun, 11am to 8pm Thu & Fri) features harbor views, soups, salads and sandwiches. Further down the waterfront, the Barking Crab (p67) is great for seafood and drinks.

A B C D

1

New Sudbury St

Bowdoin

Cambridge St

Haymarket

John F Fitzgerald Surface Rd

13

City Hall Plaza

Boston City Hall

Faneuil Hall

14

Atlantic Ave

Rose Kennedy Greenway

6

24

Aquariu

Government Center

National Park Service Visitors Center

5

Quincy Market

Joy St

Hancock St

Bowdoin St

Somerset St

Myrtle St

Massachusetts State House

Boston Harbor Islands Pavilion

Court St

Old State House

1

State

Old State House

Mt Vernon St

King's Chapel & Burying Ground

4

State St

Kilby St

Water St

India St

Purchase St

Atlantic Ave

Beacon St

Park St

Tremont St

School St

19

DOWNTOWN

Broad St

Batterymarch St

High St

22

2

16

Old South Meeting House

2

Liberty Square

Milk St

Devonshire St

Franklin St

Pearl St

Oliver St

Wharf District Parks

Park St

Downtown Crossing

Winter St

Hawley St

Federal St

Temple Pl

23

West St

Washington St

Macy's

Arch St

Otis St

Matthews St

High St

Boston Common

21

Chauncy St

Summer St

Dewey Sq Parks

Congress St

Boston Te Party Ship & Museum

3

17

Avery St

Millennium Place

Ave de Lafayette

20

Bedford St

Kingston St

One Financial Place

South Station

Atlantic Ave

Congress St

Congress St Bridge

Boylston St

Boylston

Essex St

Chinatown

Kingston St

Tufts St

South Station

US South Boston Postal Annex

Summer St

Summer St Bridge

THEATER DISTRICT

Beach St

LEATHER DISTRICT

Stuart St

Tufts Medical Center

Harrison Ave

Tyler St

Hudson St

Surface Rd

Kneeland St

Lincoln St

Dorchester Ave

Necco Ct

Tremont St

Washington St

Harvard St

CHINATOWN

Oak St W

Marginal Rd

Fort Point Channel

Massachusetts Turnpike

5

E   F   G   H

$$\overset{N}{\bigcirc} \quad \begin{matrix} 0 & & & \text{500 m} \\ 0 & & & \text{0.25 miles} \end{matrix}$$

1

For reviews see

◉	Top Sights	p58
◉	Sights	p64
✖	Eating	p66
🍸	Drinking	p68
★	Entertainment	p70
🛍	Shopping	p71

WATERFRONT

New England
Aquarium
8 ◉

New England
Aquarium
Whale Watch

Boston Inner Harbor

2

Old Northern
Ave Bridge   Harbour Walk

Evelyn   Fan
Moakley   Moakley Federal   Pier
Bridge ✖12   Courthouse

Institute of
Contemporary
Art ◉

Northern Ave   Marine Park Dr

3

Sleeper St

World
Trade
Center

Boston
Children's   P
Museum

Thomson Pl
Stillings St
Boston Wharf Rd

SEAPORT
DISTRICT   P

Fish
Pier

Commonwealth
Pier

4

✖15

E. Service Rd

Seaport Blvd

B St

Summer St   9✖

Congress St

W Service Rd

11 ✖

10 ✖

Boston Convention
& Exhibition Center

18 ◉

5

Sights

Old State House   HISTORIC BUILDING

1 ◎ Map p62, C2

Dating to 1713, the Old State House is Boston's oldest surviving public building, where the Massachusetts Assembly used to debate the issues of the day before the revolution. The building is best known for its balcony, where the Declaration of Independence was first read to Bostonians in 1776. Inside, the Old State House contains a small museum of revolutionary memorabilia, with videos and multimedia presentations about the Boston Massacre (p48), which took place out front. (www.bostonhistory.org; 206 Washington St; adult/child $10/free; ⊙9am-6pm Jun-Aug, to 5pm Sep-May; ⓣState)

Old South Meeting House   HISTORIC BUILDING

2 ◎ Map p62, C2

'No tax on tea!' That was the decision on December 16, 1773, when 5000 angry colonists gathered here to protest British taxes, leading to the Boston Tea Party (p67). Download an audio of the historic pre–Tea Party meeting from the museum website, then visit the graceful meeting house to check out the exhibit on the history of the building and the protest. (www.osmh.org; 310 Washington St; adult/child $6/1; ⊙9:30am-5pm Apr-Oct, 10am-4pm Nov-Mar; ♿; ⓣDowntown Crossing, State)

Boston Tea Party Ships & Museum   MUSEUM

3 ◎ Map p62, D4

'Boston Harbor a teapot tonight!' To protest unfair taxes, a gang of rebellious colonists dumped 342 chests of tea into the water. The 1773 protest – the Boston Tea Party – set into motion the events leading to the Revolutionary War. Nowadays, replica Tea Party Ships are moored at Griffin's Wharf, alongside an excellent experiential museum dedicated to the catalytic event. Using reenactments, multimedia and other fun exhibits, the museum addresses all aspects of the Boston Tea Party and the events that followed. (www.bostonteapartyship. com; Congress St Bridge; adult/child $28/18; ⊙10am-5pm; ♿; ⓣSouth Station)

King's Chapel & Burying Ground   CHURCH, CEMETERY

4 ◎ Map p62, B2

Puritan Bostonians were not pleased when the original Anglican church was erected on this site in 1688. The granite chapel standing today – built in 1754 – houses the largest bell ever made by Paul Revere, as well as a historic organ. The adjacent burying ground is the oldest in the city. Besides the biweekly services, recitals are held here every week (12:15pm Tuesday). (www.kings-chapel.org; 58 Tremont St; donation $2, Bells & Bones tour adult/child $10/5; ⊙church 10am-5pm Mon-Sat, 1:30-5pm Sun, hourly tours 11am-3pm except noon; ⓣGovernment Center)

Old State House

Faneuil Hall
HISTORIC BUILDING

5 ◎ Map p62, C1

'Those who cannot bear free speech had best go home,' said Wendell Phillips. 'Faneuil Hall is no place for slavish hearts.' Indeed, this public meeting place was the site of so much rabble-rousing that it earned the nickname the 'Cradle of Liberty.' After the revolution, Faneuil Hall was a forum for meetings about abolition, women's suffrage and war. On the 2nd floor, the historic hall is normally open to the public, who can hear about the building's history from National Park Service (NPS) rangers. (www.nps.gov/bost; Congress St; admission free; ⊘9am-5pm; T State, Haymarket, Government Center)

Rose Kennedy Greenway
PARK

6 ◎ Map p62, D1

The gateway to the newly revitalized waterfront is the Rose Kennedy Greenway. Where once was a hulking overhead highway, now winds a 27-acre strip of landscaped gardens, fountain-lined greens and public art installations, with the artist-driven Greenway Open Market (p71) for weekend shoppers, food trucks for weekday lunchers and a brand-new European-style beer garden, which made its debut in 2017. Cool off in the whimsical **Rings Fountain** (T Aquarium), walk the calming **labyrinth** (ⵐ; T Haymarket), or take a ride on the custom-designed **Greenway Carousel** (per ride $3; ⊙11am-7pm Apr-Dec; ♿; T Aquarium). (www.rosekennedygreenway. org; ♿; T Aquarium, Haymarket)

Boston Children's Museum

MUSEUM

7 ◎ Map p62, E4

The interactive, educational exhibits at the delightful Boston Children's Museum keep kids entertained for hours. Highlights include a bubble exhibit, rock-climbing walls, a hands-on construction site and intercultural immersion experiences. The light-filled atrium features an amazing three-story climbing maze. In nice weather kids can enjoy outdoor eating and playing in the waterside park. Look for the iconic Hood milk bottle on Fort Point Channel. (www.bostonchildrensmuseum.org; 308 Congress St; $16, Fri 5-9pm $1; ⊙10am-5pm Sat-Thu, to 9pm Fri; ♿; T South Station)

New England Aquarium Whale Watch

WHALE WATCHING

8 ◎ Map p62, E2

Set off from Long Wharf for the journey to Stellwagen Bank, a rich feeding ground for whales, dolphins and marine birds. Keen-eyed boat captains and onboard naturalists can answer all your questions and have been trained by New England Aquarium experts to ensure that the tours do not interfere with the animals or harm them in any way. (☎617-227-4321; www.neaq.org/exhibits/whale-watch; Central Wharf; adult/child/infant $53/33/16; ⊙times vary late Mar–mid-Nov; T Aquarium)

Eating

Row 34

SEAFOOD $$

9 ✕ Map p62, E4

In the heart of the new Seaport District, set in a sharp, postindustrial space, this place offers a dozen types of raw oysters and clams, alongside an amazing selection of craft beers. There's also a full menu of cooked seafood, ranging from the traditional to

---

Q **Local Life**

Downtown Lunch Break

Where do locals go on their lunch break? **Casa Razdora** (Map p62, C2; www.casarazdora.com; 115 Water St; mains $7-13; ⊙11am-4pm Mon-Wed, to 5pm Thu & Fri; ✐; T State) is a perennial favorite for housemade pasta topped with fresh sauces. **Falafel King** (Map p62, B2 www.falafelkingofboston.com; 260 Washington St; mains $6-9; ⊙11am-8pm Mon-Fri, to 6pm Sat & Sun; ✐; T State) and **Clover Food Lab** (Map p62, B2; www.cloverfoodlab.com; 27 School St; mains $8-12; ⊙7am-11pm Mon-Fri, 8am-11pm Sat, 8am-8pm Sun; ✐; T State) serve up fast Middle Eastern and vegetarian fare, respectively. For good old-fashioned sandwiches, head to **Sam La Grassa's** (Map p62, B2; www.samlagrassas.com; 44 Province St; sandwiches $13-14; ⊙11am-3:30pm Mon-Fri; ✐; T Downtown Crossing).

Understand
Boston Tea Party

In May 1773 the British Parliament passed the Tea Act, granting a trade monopoly to the East India Company and requiring colonists to pay additional taxes on their tea. In December three tea-bearing vessels arrived in Boston Harbor, but colonial merchants refused the shipments. When they tried to depart, Governor Hutchinson demanded their cargo be unloaded.

At a meeting in the Old South Church, the Sons of Liberty decided to take matters into their own hands. Disguised as Mohawk Indians, they descended on the waterfront, boarded the ships and dumped 90,000lb of taxable tea into the harbor.

The king's retribution was swift. Legislation was rushed through Parliament to punish Boston, 'the center of rebellious commotion in America, the ring leader in every riot.' The port was blockaded and the city placed under military rule, which further fueled tensions between colonists and the king.

the trendy. (☎617-553-5900; www.row34. com; 383 Congress St; oysters $2-3, mains $13-29; ⏰11:30am-10pm Sun-Thu, to 11pm Fri & Sat; Ⓣ South Station)

Yankee Lobster Co   SEAFOOD $

10 🍴 Map p62, H5

The Zanti family has been fishing for three generations, so they definitely know their stuff. A relatively recent addition is this retail fish market, scattered with a few tables in case you want to dine in. And you do. Order something simple like clam chowder or a lobster roll, accompany it with a cold beer, and you will not be disappointed. (www.yankeelobstercompany.com; 300 Northern Ave; mains $10-25; ⏰10am-9pm Mon-Sat, 11am-6pm Sun; 🚌SL1, SL2, Ⓣ South Station)

Legal Harborside   SEAFOOD $$

11 🍴 Map p62, G5

This vast glass-fronted waterfront complex offers three different restaurant concepts on three floors. Our favorite is the 1st floor – a casual restaurant and fish market that is a throwback to Legal's original outlet from 1904. The updated menu includes a raw bar, small plates, seafood grills and plenty of international influences. There is outdoor seating in the summer months. (www.legalseafoods.com; 270 Northern Ave; mains $14-30; ⏰11am-10pm Sun-Thu, to 11pm Fri & Sat; 🚌SL1, SL2, Ⓣ South Station)

Barking Crab   SEAFOOD $$

12 🍴 Map p62, E3

Big buckets of crabs (bairdi, Alaskan, snow, Dungeness etc), steamers (steamed clams) dripping in lemon and butter, paper plates piled high with all things fried, pitchers of ice-cold beer... Devour your feast at communal picnic tables overlooking the water. Service is slack, noise levels are high, but the atmosphere is jovial. Prepare to wait for a table if the weather is warm. (www.barkingcrab. com; 88 Sleeper St; sandwiches $12-18, mains $18-32; ⏱11:30am-10pm Sun-Wed, to 11pm Thu-Sat; 🚌SL1, SL2, ⓣSouth Station)

Union Oyster House   SEAFOOD $$$

13 🍴 Map p62, C1

The oldest restaurant in Boston, ye olde Union Oyster House has been serving seafood in this historic redbrick building since 1826. Countless historymakers have propped themselves up at this bar, including Daniel Webster and John F Kennedy (apparently JFK used to order the lobster bisque). Overpriced but atmospheric. (www.unionoysterhouse.com; 41 Union St; mains lunch $14-26, dinner $22-32; ⏱11am-9:30pm Sun-Thu, to 10pm Fri & Sat; ⓣHaymarket)

Quincy Market   FOOD HALL $

14 🍴 Map p62, C1

Behind Faneuil Hall, this food court offers a variety of places under one roof: the place is packed with about 20 restaurants and 40 food stalls. Choose from chowder, bagels, ice cream, hot dogs etc, and take a seat at one of the tables in the central rotunda. It's usually crowded and

mostly overpriced, but it sure is convenient. (www.faneuilhallmarketplace.com; Congress St; ⏱10am-9pm Mon-Sat, noon-6pm Sun; 🛜 ✒; ⓣHaymarket, Aquarium)

Drinking

Drink   COCKTAIL BAR

15 🍸 Map p62, E4

There is no cocktail menu at Drink. Instead you have a chat with the bartender, and he or she will whip something up according to your specifications. It takes seriously the art of drink mixology – and you will too, after you sample one of its concoctions. The subterranean space, with its low-lit, sexy ambience, makes a great date destination. (www.drinkfortpoint.com; 348 Congress St; ⏱4pm-1am; 🚌SL1, SL2, ⓣSouth Station)

Highball Lounge   COCKTAIL BAR

16 🍸 Map p62, B2

Go out to play! Well stocked with board games, the Highball Lounge has yours, whether you're on a date (Connect Four) or in a group (Jenga). The Viewmaster is for looking at the menu, which features local beers, creative cocktails and intriguing snacks (tater-tot nachos, crispy brussel sprouts). This place will make you feel like a kid again. Except you can drink. (www.highballboston.com; 90 Tremont St; ⏱5pm-midnight Mon & Tue, 2am Wed-Sat; ⓣPark St)

Understand

Seafood

A word to the wise: when in Boston, eat as much seafood as possible. Here's a quick guide to the New England classics.

Chowder
Ask 10 locals for Boston's best chowder and you'll get 10 different answers. This thick, cream-based soup is chock-full of clams or fish, although clam chowder, using the meaty insides of giant surf clams, is more prevalent. Sample it at Union Oyster House.

Clams & Oysters
Many seafood restaurants showcase their shellfish at a raw bar, where a dedicated bartender works to shuck raw oysters and clams to be served on the half-shell. Any self-respecting raw bar will have a selection of hard-shelled clams, or 'quahogs,' including littlenecks and cherrystones. The most famous type of oysters are Wellfleet oysters from Cape Cod; they're eaten raw, with a dollop of cocktail sauce and a few drops of lemon juice. For your own raw bar experience, head to Row 34 (p66). You can also get clams deep-fried or steamed (aka 'steamers').

Lobster
Back in the day, the seemingly endless supply of lobster was the food of poor people and prisoners. Now seafood lovers pay big bucks for these crustaceans. Traditionally, lobsters are steamed or boiled; then it's up to the hungry patron to crack the shell to get the succulent meat out. A less labor-intensive choice is a lobster roll, where the lobster meat is dressed with a little mayonnaise and stuffed into a grilled buttered hot-dog roll. Either way, you can't go wrong at Yankee Lobster Co (p67).

Fish
Atlantic codfish has played such an important role in the region's culture and economy that a carved wooden effigy, known as the 'sacred cod,' hangs in the Massachusetts State House. Cod, haddock, hake and other white-fleshed fish are sometimes called 'scrod.' Other fresh local fish appearing on Boston menus in summer include bluefin tuna, bluefish and striped bass, eg at Atlantic Fish Co (p99).

Thinking Cup   CAFE

17 🚇 Map p62, A3

There are a few things that make
the Thinking Cup special. One is
the French hot chocolate – *ooh la la*.
Another is the Stumptown Coffee, the
Portland brew that has earned accolades from coffee drinkers around the
country. But the best thing? It's across
from the Boston Common, making it
a perfect stop for a post–Frog Pond
warm-up. (www.thinkingcup.com; 165
Tremont St; ⏰7am-10pm Mon-Wed, to 11pm
Thu-Sun; Ⓣ Boylston)

Harpoon Brewery &
Beer Hall   BREWERY

18 🚇 Map p62, H5

This brewery is the largest beer facil-
ity in the state of Massachusetts. Take
an hour-long tour ($5) to see how the
beer is made and to sample some of
the goods. Or just take a seat at the
bar in the beer hall and watch the
action from above. (www.harpoonbrewery.
com; 306 Northern Ave; ⏰beer hall 11am-7pm
Sun-Wed, to 11pm Thu-Sat, tours noon-5pm
Mon-Wed, to 6pm Thu-Sat, 11:30am-5:30pm
Sun; 🚌SL1, SL2, Ⓣ South Station)

Last Hurrah   BAR

19 🚇 Map p62, B2

It's now named for the 1956 novel
about former Boston mayor James Mi-
chael Curley, but the elegant lobby bar
of the Omni Parker House hotel was
a hallowed haunt for Boston's 19th-
century intelligentsia and politicians.
Enjoy a dish of hot nuts and drink
a bourbon at this throwback to Old
Boston. (www.omnihotels.com; 60 School St;
⏰4pm-1am Mon-Sat; Ⓣ Park St)

Good Life   CLUB

20 🚇 Map p62, B3

The Good Life means a lot of things
to a lot of people – solid lunch option,
after-work hangout, trivia-night place
etc. But the top reason to come to the
Good Life is to get your groove on.
There are three bars and two dance
floors, with great DJs spinning tunes
Thursday to Saturday (cover $10 to
$15). (www.goodlifebar.com; 28 Kingston St;
⏰11am-midnight Mon-Wed, 11am-2am Thu &
Fri, 4pm-2am Sat; Ⓣ Downtown Crossing)

Ⓠ Local Life
Lucky's Lounge

You know it's a local hangout when
they don't bother to put a sign
outside. **Lucky's Lounge** (Map
p62, C1; http://luckyslounge.com; 355
Congress St; ⏰11:30am-2am Mon-Fri,
10am-2am Sat & Sun; 🚌SL1, SL2,
Ⓣ South Station) is a delightfully
gritty place straight out of 1959.
Don't miss the excellent martinis
and Sinatra-themed Sundays.

Entertainment

Opera House   LIVE PERFORMANCE

21 ⭐ Map p62, B3

This lavish theater has been restored
to its 1928 glory, complete with

mural-painted ceiling, gilded molding and plush velvet curtains. The glitzy venue regularly hosts productions from the Broadway Across America series, and is also the main performance space for the Boston Ballet. (www.bostonoperahouse.com; 539 Washington St; T Downtown Crossing)

Shopping

Greenway Open Market
ARTS & CRAFTS

22 🔒 Map p62, D2

This weekend artist market brings out dozens of vendors to display their wares in the open air. Look for unique, handmade gifts, jewelry, bags, paintings, ceramics and other arts and crafts – most of which are locally and ethically made. Food trucks are always on hand to cater to the hungry. (www. newenglandopenmarkets.com; Rose Kennedy Greenway; ⊙11am-5pm Sat, plus 1st & 3rd Sun May-Oct; 🛜; T Aquarium)

Brattle Book Shop
BOOKS

23 🔒 Map p62, B3

Since 1825, the Brattle Book Shop has catered to Boston's literati: it's a treasure trove crammed with out-of-print, rare and 1st edition books. Ken Gloss – whose family has owned this gem since 1949 – is an expert on antiquarian

Q Local Life
The Lawn on D

One of South Boston's coolest new hangouts, **the Lawn on D** (www.signatureboston.com/lawn-on-d; 420 D St; ⊙variable; 🚊SL1, SL2) – a vast green space and adjacent tented area – hosts a variety of special events each summer, featuring food, drink, movie nights, games and live music. At the heart of the experience is SwingTime, a set of glow-in-the-dark 'swings for adults', lit by multicolored, solar-powered LEDs.

books, moonlighting as a consultant and appraiser (see him on *Antiques Roadshow*). Don't miss the bargains on the outside lot. (www.brattlebookshop.com; 9 West St; ⊙9am-5:30pm Mon-Sat; T Park St, Downtown Crossing)

Lucy's League
CLOTHING

24 🔒 Map p62, D1

Sometimes a girl wants to look good while she's supporting the team. At Lucy's League, fashionable sports fans will find shirts, jackets and other gear sporting the local teams' logos in supercute styles designed to flatter the female figure. (www.rosterstores.com/lucysleague; North Market, Faneuil Hall; ⊙10am-9pm Mon-Sat, to 7pm Sun; T State)

Top Sights
Boston Harbor Islands

Getting There

Boston Harbor Cruises offers seasonal ferry service (adult/child $17/10) from Long Wharf to Georges Island or Spectacle Island, where you catch other boats to the smaller islands.

Boston Harbor is sprinkled with 34 islands, many of which are open for trail walking, bird-watching, fishing, swimming and camping. The islands offer a range of ecosystems – sandy beaches, rocky cliffs, fresh- and saltwater marshes, and forested trails – only 45 minutes from downtown Boston. Since the massive, multi-million-dollar cleanup of Boston Harbor in the mid-1990s, the islands have become one of the city's most magnificent natural assets.

Georges Island

Boston Harbor Islands Pavilion

Ideally located on the Rose Kennedy Greenway, this **information center** (Map p62; www.bostonharborislands.org; Rose Kennedy Greenway; ⊙9am-4:30pm mid-May–Jun & Sep-early Oct, to 6pm Jul & Aug; 🖥; ⊤Aquarium) will tell you everything you need to know to plan your visit to the Boston Harbor Islands.

Georges Island

Georges Island is one of the transportation hubs for the Boston Harbor Islands. It is also the site of Fort Warren, a 19th-century fort and Civil War prison. While National Park Service (NPS) rangers give guided tours of the fort and there is a small museum, it is largely abandoned, with many dark tunnels, creepy corners and magnificent lookouts to discover.

Spectacle Island

A Harbor Islands hub, **Spectacle Island** (⊙dawn-dusk early May–mid-Sep; 🚻; 🖥from Long Wharf) has a large marina, a solar-powered visitor center, a healthy snack bar and sandy, supervised beaches. Five miles of walking trails provide access to a 157ft peak overlooking the harbor. Special events include Sunday-afternoon jazz concerts and Thursday-evening clam bakes. Ferries run here directly from Long Wharf.

Lovells Island

With camping and picnicking facilities, Lovells is one of the most popular Harbor Islands destinations. Two deadly shipwrecks may bode badly for seafarers, but that doesn't seem to stop recreational boaters, swimmers and sunbathers from lounging on Lovells' long rocky beach. European settlers once used the island as a rabbit run, and until recently descendent bunnies were still running this place.

www.bostonharborislands.org

⊙9am-dusk mid-Apr–mid-Oct

🖥from Long Wharf

☑ Top Tips

▶ Don't try to visit more than two islands in one day: you'll end up spending all your time riding on or waiting for boats – though the boat ride is half of the fun in an island park!

▶ Check the website (www.bostonharborislands.org) for special events, such as live music, outdoor activities and other family programs on Georges and Spectacle Islands.

✕ Take a Break

Georges and Spectacle Islands have snack shacks (open from 10am to 5pm) but there is no food or water on the other islands. Pack a picnic!

Harbor Islands in a Day

Hop on the first ferry to Georges Island, where you can spend the morning exploring historic Fort Warren. After lunch, take the shuttle to one of the other islands. Hit Spectacle Island for good walking trails and marvelous city views. Head to Lovells to catch some rays and cool off in the refreshing harbor waters. Or venture to Grape Island to hunt for wild berries.

Catch a ferry back to the mainland via Spectacle or Georges.

Bumpkin Island

The beaches at Bumpkin are not the best for swimming, as they are slate and seashell – but there's a network of trails through fields overgrown with wildflowers, leading to the remains of an old stone farmhouse and an old hospital. It's one of four islands with camping facilities.

Grape Island

Grape Island is rich with fruity goodness. An arbor decked with cultivated grapes greets you opposite the boat dock, while the wild raspberries, bayberries and elderberries growing along the island's scrubby wooded trails attract abundant birdlife. The island also offers a few campsites.

Peddocks Island

One of the largest Harbor Islands, Peddocks consists of four headlands connected by sandbars. Hiking trails wander through marsh, pond and coastal environs, and around the remains of Fort Andrews. There are campsites and yurts if you fancy an overnight stay.

Little Brewster Island

Little Brewster is the country's oldest light station and site of the iconic Boston Light, dating from 1783. Make reservations for an organized **tour** (📞617-223-8666; adult/youth/nonclimber $41/32/30; 🕑9:30am & 1pm Fri-Sun Jun-Sep; ⛴from Long Wharf), where you'll learn about Boston's maritime history during a one-hour sail around the harbor, then spend two hours exploring the island.

Thompson Island

Thompson Island was settled as early as 1626 by a Scotsman, David Thompson, who set up a trading post to do business with the Neponset Indians. Today this island is privately owned by Thompson Island Outward Bound, a nonprofit organization that develops fun and challenging physical adventures, especially for training and developing leadership skills. The public can explore its 200-plus acres only on weekends, when it's wonderful for walking, fishing and birding.

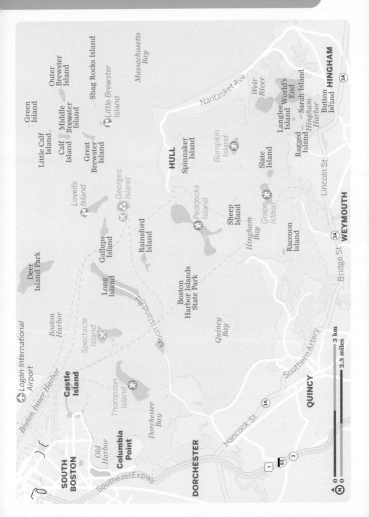

Mussachusetts Bay

Outer Brewster Island

Shag Rocks Island

Green Island

Middle Brewster Island

Little Brewster Island

Little Calf Island

Calf Island

Great Brewster Island

Weir River

Nantasket Ave

Langlee World's Island End

Sarah Island

HINGHAM

Button Island

3A

HULL

Spinnaker Island

Bumpkin Island

Hingham Harbor

Ragged Island

Slate Island

Georges Island

Lovells Island

Peddocks Island

Sheep Island

Lincoln St

Gallups Island

Rainsford Island

Hingham Bay

Grape Island

Raccoon Island

Deer Island Park

Boston Harbor

Long Island

Boston Harbor Islands State Park

Quincy Bay

Bridge St

3A

WEYMOUTH

Logan International Airport

Spectacle Island

Moon Island

Southern Artery

Boston Inner Harbor

Castle Island

Thompson Island

Dorchester Bay

QUINCY

SOUTH BOSTON

Old Harbor

Columbia Point

Hancock St

3A

DORCHESTER

Southeast Expwy

1

93

3

5 km

2.5 miles

N

禮義廉恥

Explore

South End & Chinatown

Chinatown, the Theater District and the Leather District are overlapping areas, filled with glitzy theaters, Chinese restaurants and the remnants of Boston's shoe and leather industry (now converted lofts and clubs). Nearby, the Victorian manses in the South End have been reclaimed by artists and gays, who have created a vibrant restaurant and gallery scene.

The Sights in a Day

☀️ These four side-by-side neighborhoods do not really contain any traditional 'sights,' but they are home to Boston's lively theater scene, its most hip-hop-happening nightclubs and its best international and contemporary dining. To check it out, head first to the South End for shopping along Tremont St.

☀️ Take lunch at the **South End Buttery** (p79). In the afternoon, you can explore the galleries in the SoWa art district.

🌙 For dinner, you'll have to choose between something contemporary and cool in the South End, such as **Coppa** (p82), or something authentically Asian in Chinatown, such as the **Gourmet Dumpling House** (p82). Afterwards, treat yourself to a show in the Theater District or dance the night away at **Candi** (p86).

For a local's day in the South End, see p78.

🔍 **Local Life**

South End Art Stroll (p78)

💜 **Best of Boston**

Eating
Gourmet Dumpling House (p82)

Coppa (p82)

Myers & Chang (p82)

Drinking
Beehive (p84)

Delux Café (p84)

Shopping
Bobby from Boston (p87)

SoWa Open Market (p82)

Getting There

🚇 **Metro** The orange line is the most useful, with stops at Chinatown, Back Bay and Tufts Medical Center.

🚌 **Bus** Good for the South End, the silver line bus runs down Washington St from South Station (SL4) or Downtown Crossing (SL5).

Local Life
South End Art Stroll

Boston's main art district is the South End. The artistic community has moved into the once-barren area south of Washington St (now known as SoWa), converting old warehouses into studios and galleries. For best results, do this walk on a summer weekend (May to October) or in the evening on the first Friday of the month (year-round).

1 SoWa Artists Guild

This is the epicenter of the South End art scene, where artists have carved out studios and gallery space from the former factories on Harrison Ave. The **SoWa Artists Guild** (www.sowaartistsguild. com; 450 Harrison Ave; ⊙5-9pm 1st Fri of month; ⊒SL4, SL5, T Tufts Medical Center) hosts an Open Studios event on the first Friday of every month, and in summer the streets fill with food trucks, a beer garden and outdoor markets.

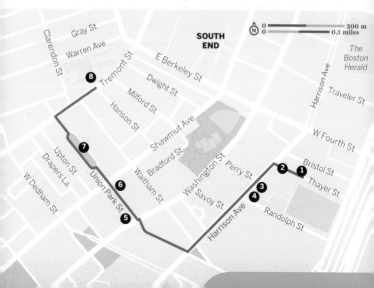

2 Thayer Street Galleries

There are dozens of arts-focused venues in the former warehouses along pedestrianized Thayer St, including **Bromfield Art Gallery** (www.bromfieldgallery.com; 450 Harrison Ave; ⊘noon-5pm Wed-Sun; 🚍SL4, SL5, Ⓣ Tufts Medical Center), a long-established artist-run gallery that features New England artists.

3 Boston Sculptors Gallery

Dedicated to three-dimensional art in all media, this innovative cooperative **gallery** (www.bostonsculptors.com; 486 Harrison Ave; ⊘noon-6pm Wed-Sun; Ⓣ Tufts Medical Center) has been going strong for over 25 years. Peek inside and meet some of the three dozen local artists who run it.

4 Ars Libri

Ring the doorbell: **Ars Libri** (www.arslibri.com; 500 Harrison Ave; ⊘9am-6pm Mon-Fri, 11am-5pm Sat; 🚍SL4, SL5, Ⓣ Tufts Medical Center) is an art bookstore extraordinaire, specializing in rare and out-of-print books. The former warehouse is filled from floor to ceiling with books on all aspects and eras of art, architecture and design.

5 The Gallows

Turn up Washington St and into the **Gallows** (Map p80, C5; www.thegallowsboston.com; 1395 Washington St; ⊘4-11pm Mon-Wed, noon-midnight Thu, noon-1am Fri, 11am-1am Sat, 11am-11pm Sun; 🚍SL4, SL5, Ⓣ Tufts Medical Center). It's hard to say whether it's a restaurant with amazing cocktails

and a cozy, convivial atmosphere, or a pub with irresistible, innovative food. It's a fave among trendy, friendly South Enders.

6 South End Buttery

If it's too early for drinks and appetizers, head up the street to the **South End Buttery** (www.southendbuttery.com; 314 Shawmut Ave; mains cafe $4-13, brunch $11-17, dinner $18-25; ⊘6am-9pm Sun-Thu, to 10pm Fri & Sat; 🖉; 🚍SL4 or SL5, Ⓣ Back Bay) for coffee and cupcakes. A portion of revenue goes to a local animal shelter, coffee drinks feature shade-grown organic beans, and packaging materials are made from recycled paper. Now that your conscience is eased, indulge!

7 Union Park

Continue up Union Park St to get a glimpse of the neighborhood's charming Victorian rowhouses, clustered around a tree-lined, fountain-filled park. This is South End architecture at its best.

8 Boston Center for the Arts

Finish your walk at the **Boston Center for the Arts** (www.bcaonline.org; 539 Tremont St; Ⓣ Back Bay), home to several performing-arts venues as well as the **Mills Gallery** (www.bcaonline.org; 551 Tremont St; ⊘noon-5pm Wed & Sun, to 9pm Thu-Sat; Ⓣ Back Bay), which hosts cutting-edge visual-arts exhibits and talks.

First Baptist Church

Newbury St

Arlington 🅣

Four Seasons Hotel

THEATER DISTRICT

Park Plaza

State Transportation Building

Boylston St

Providence St

Arlington St

Columbus Ave

500 Boylston St

St James Ave

Berkeley St

Statler Park

Radisson Hotel

🅣 Copley

Copley Square

Charles St S

John Hancock Tower

Trinity Pl

Clarendon St

Stuart St

Park Plaza Castle

Piedmont St

Winchester St

Melrose St

Charles St S

Isabella St

BAY VILLAGE

Fayette St

🅧 5

Cortes St

Tremont S

Massachusetts Turnpike 🛣 90

Marginal Rd

🅣 Back Bay/ South End

Dartmouth St

Columbus Ave

Chandler St

Berkeley St

Paul Pl

Tent City

Yarmouth St

Lawrence St

Gray St

SOUTH END

15
🅧

Appleton St

Dartmouth Pl

17
🅓

E Berkeley St

9
🅟

Dwight St

Warren Ave

Milford St

Hanson St

2 🅧

W Canton St

Montgomery St

18 🅓

Tremont St

6
🅧

1
🅧

Shawmut Ave

Bradford St

Washington St

Perry St

W Brookline St

Upton St

Drapers La

W Dedham St

Union Park St

Waltham St

Savoy St

8
🔺🅓🅧

81

E   F   G   H

Colonial Theatre
Boylston
Chinatown
Essex St
Oxford St
LEATHER DISTRICT
South Station

LaGrange St
3
Chinatown Park
Tufts St
East St
12

10
7
Stuart St
CHINATOWN
Beach St
Ulica St
South St
Atlantic Ave

14

13
Wang Theatre
Tyler St
Surface Rd
Beach St

11
Shawmut Ave
Tufts Medical Center
Harvard St
Hudson St
Lincoln St
Kneeland St

2
US South Boston Postal Annex

Ash St
Harrison Ave
Oak St W
Washington St

Pine St

3
Dorchester Ave
Fort Point Channel

Herald St

Broadway

The Boston Herald
Bass River
Broadway

4

Harrison Ave
Traveler St

W Broadway

Harrison Ave
W Fourth St
93
1

16
Bristol St
Thayer St
Randolph St

For reviews see
🍴 Eating   p82
🍷 Drinking   p84
🎭 Entertainment p86
🛍 Shopping   p87

5

N 0   400 m
   0   0.2 miles

Eating

Coppa   ITALIAN $$

1 🍴 Map p80, C5

This South End *enoteca* (wine bar) re-creates an Italian dining experience with authenticity and innovation, serving up *salumi* (cured meats), antipasti, pasta and other delicious small plates. Wash it all down with an Aperol spritz and you might be tricked into thinking you're in Venice.

☑️ Top Tip

Weekends in the South End

Summer Saturdays and Sundays are lively in the South End. Three different markets fill the art district's parking lots: the **SoWa Open Market** (Map p80, E5; www.sowaboston.com; Thayer St; ⏱10am-4pm Sat & Sun May-Oct; 🚇SL4, SL5, 🚇Tufts Medical Center) for arts and crafts, **SoWa Farmers Market** (Map p80, E5; www.sowaboston.com; 500 Harrison Ave; ⏱10am-4pm Sat & Sun May-Oct) for fresh produce and **SoWa Vintage Market** (Map p80, E5; www.sowavintagemarket.com; 450 Harrison Ave; ⏱10am-4pm Sun year-round, plus 5-9pm 1st Fri of month & 11am-4pm Sat May-Oct) for antique treasures. Right next door at 540 Harrison Ave, you'll find a fabulous Food Truck Bazaar and a summer beer garden.

(📞617-391-0902; www.coppaboston.com; 253 Shawmut Ave; small plates $5-15, pizza & pasta $14-26; ⏱noon-10pm Mon-Thu, noon-11pm Fri, 11am-11pm Sat, 11am-10pm Sun; 🚇SL4, SL5, 🚇Back Bay)

Myers & Chang   ASIAN $$

2 🍴 Map p80, D4

This superhip Asian spot blends Thai, Chinese and Vietnamese cuisines, which means delicious dumplings, spicy stir-fries and oodles of noodles. The kitchen staff do amazing things with a wok, and the menu of small plates allows you to sample a wide selection of dishes. Dim sum for dinner? This is your place. (📞617-542-5200; www.myersandchang.com; 1145 Washington St; small plates $9-19; ⏱11:30am-10pm Sun-Thu, to 11pm Fri & Sat; 🍷; 🚇SL4, SL5, 🚇Tufts Medical Center)

Gourmet Dumpling House

CHINESE, TAIWANESE $

3 🍴 Map p80, F1

Xiao long bao. That's all the Chinese you need to know to take advantage of the specialty at the Gourmet Dumpling House (or GDH, as it is fondly called). They are Shanghai soup dumplings, and they are fresh, doughy and delicious. The menu offers plenty of other options, including scrumptious crispy scallion pancakes. Come early or be prepared to wait. (52 Beach St; dumplings $4-9, mains $9-21; ⏱11am-11:30pm; 🍷; 🚇Chinatown)

Paella, Toro

Toro TAPAS $$

4 Map p80, C5

True to its Spanish spirit, Toro is bursting with energy, from the open kitchen to the lively bar to the communal butcher-block tables. The menu features simple but sublime tapas – grilled chilies with sea salt, corn on the cob dripping with lemon and butter, and delectable, garlicky shrimp. For accompaniment, take your pick from rioja, sangria or its spiced-up mojitos and margaritas. (✆617-536-4300; www.toro-restaurant.com; 1704 Washington St; tapas $9-16; ⓦnoon-10:15pm Mon-Thu, noon-11:45pm Fri, 5-11:45pm Sat, 10:30am-10:15pm Sun; ⚲; ⧮SL4, SL5, Ⓣ Massachusetts Ave)

Mike & Patty's SANDWICHES $

5 Map p80, D2

Tucked away in Bay Village, this hole-in-the-wall gem of a corner sandwich shop does amazing things between two slices of bread. There are only eight options and they're all pretty perfect, but the hands-down favorite is the Fancy (fried egg, cheddar cheese, bacon and avocado on multigrain). There's always a line but it moves quickly. (www.mikeandpattys.com; 12 Church St; sandwiches $5-11; ⓦ8am-2pm; ⚲; Ⓣ Tufts Medical Center, Arlington)

Butcher Shop

FRENCH, ITALIAN $$

6   Map p80, B4

Only in the South End does the neighborhood butcher shop double as an elegant eatery and wine bar. The cases filled with tantalizing cuts of meat, fresh foie gras and homemade sausages give a glimpse of the ingredients and provide the decoration at this bistro (not a good place for vegetarians). There is a nice selection of artisanal wines. (☎617-423-4800; www.thebutchershopboston.com; 552 Tremont St; mains $14-45; ⏰11:30am-11pm; Ⓣ Back Bay)

My Thai Vegan Café

THAI $

7   Map p80, F1

This welcoming cafe is up a sketchy staircase, tucked into a sunlit 2nd-story space. It's an animal-free zone – but good enough that meat eaters will enjoy eating here too. The menu has a Thai twist, offering noodle soups, dumplings, excellent spring rolls and pad Thai. The bubble tea gets rave reviews. (http://mythaivegancafe.com; 3 Beach St; mains $8-17; ⏰11am-10pm Sun-Thu, to 11pm Fri & Sat; ☝; Ⓣ Chinatown)

Drinking

Gallows

PUB

8   Map p80, C5

It's a relative newcomer, but already a South End favorite. The dark woody interior is inviting and the bartenders are truly talented. The gastropub grub includes such enticing fare as the Scotch egg (a soft-cooked egg wrapped in crispy pork sausage) and scrumptious vegetarian poutine. Solid beer selection, delectable cocktails. (www.thegallowsboston.com; 1395 Washington St; ⏰4-11pm Mon-Wed, noon-midnight Thu, noon-1am Fri, 11am-1am Sat, 11am-11pm Sun; ▣SL4, SL5, Ⓣ Tufts Medical Center)

Beehive

COCKTAIL BAR

9   Map p80, B4

The Beehive has transformed the basement of the Boston Center for the Arts into a 1920s Paris jazz club. This place is more about the scene than the music, which is often provided by students from Berklee College of Music. But the food is good and the vibe is definitely hip. Reservations required if you want a table. (☎617-423-0069; www.beehiveboston.com; 541 Tremont St; ⏰5pm-midnight Mon-Wed, to 1am Thu, to 2am Fri, 9:30am-2am Sat, 9:30am-midnight Sun; Ⓣ Back Bay)

Local Life

Delux Café

This delightful **dive bar** (Map p80, B3; ☎617-338-5258; 100 Chandler St; ⏰5pm-1am; Ⓣ Back Bay) is one of a kind. The small room on the ground floor of a brownstone comes complete with knotty pine paneling, artwork from old LPs, Christmas lights and a totally laid-back atmosphere. The kitchen turns out an incredible grilled-cheese sandwich.

Understand
Boston Depicted...

Considering Boston's rich literary tradition and its cinematic architecture, it's no surprise that the city is well represented in print and on screen.

In Print
▶ *The Scarlet Letter* (Nathaniel Hawthorne; 1850) Hypocrisy and malice in Puritan New England.

▶ *The Given Day* (Dennis Lehane; 2008) Historical novel, following two families through the turbulence of post-WWI Boston.

▶ *Interpreter of Maladies* (Jhumpa Lahiri; 1999) Pulitzer Prize-winner on the challenges of migration and multiculturalism.

▶ *The Friends of Eddie Coyle* (George Higgins; 1972) A crime novel with a crash course in the Boston dialect.

On Screen
▶ *Good Will Hunting* (1997) Put South Boston on the Hollywood map.

▶ *Next Stop Wonderland* (1997) Heartwarming independent film with a bossa nova soundtrack.

▶ *John Adams* (2008) Critically acclaimed TV series chronicling the life and times of the second US president.

▶ *The Social Network* (2010) Fictionalized drama of the founding of Facebook.

▶ *Spotlight* (2015) Riveting account of *Boston Globe* reporters uncovering child sex abuse within the Roman Catholic church.

PAUL MAROTTA/GETTY IMAGES ©

Shubert Theatre

Jacob Wirth BEER HALL

10 Map p80, E1

This atmospheric Bavarian beer hall is Boston's second-oldest eatery. The menu features Wiener schnitzel, sauerbraten, potato pancakes and pork chops, but the highlight is the beer – almost 30 different drafts, including Jake's Special Dark. From Thursday to Saturday (from 8pm), Jake hosts a sing-along that rouses the *haus*. (📞617-338-8586; www.jacobwirth.com; 31-37 Stuart St; ⊙11:30am-last guest; T Boylston, Chinatown)

Candi CLUB

11 Map p80, E2

Welcome to the future, where the walls and ceiling are covered with multicolored lights that throb in time with the music. A state-of-the-art sound system gets you moving on the dance floor. And when you need a break, you can find a seat on the shapely plastic furniture. In a word, surreal. The cover is $10 to $20. (www.candiboston.com; 279 Tremont St; ⊙10pm-2am; T Tufts Medical Center)

Entertainment

Cutler Majestic Theatre THEATER

12 ⭐ Map p80, E1

This beautiful beaux-arts-style opera house dates to 1903. A century after its construction, the theater was sumptuously renovated and reopened by Emerson College. Today, the performances here are incredibly diverse, and include music, dance, comedy, acrobatics and seasonal celebrations like the popular Celtic Christmas Sojourn. (📞617-824-8400; www.cutlermajestic.org; 219 Tremont St; T Boylston)

Shubert Theatre LIVE PERFORMANCE

13 ⭐ Map p80, E2

With 1600 seats, the Shubert is smaller and more intimate than some of the other Theater District venues, thus earning the moniker 'Little Princess.' The theater hosts a variety of performing-arts events, including touring Broadway shows, theater, music, dance and opera. (www.bochcenter.org; 265 Tremont St; T Boylston)

Wilbur Theatre   COMEDY

14 ⭐ Map p80, E1

The colonial Wilbur Theatre dates to 1914. These days it is Boston's premier comedy club. The smallish house hosts nationally known cut-ups, as well as music acts and other kinds of hard-to-categorize performances. The theater itself could do with a renovation, but the talent is good. (www.thewilbur.com; 246 Tremont St; tickets $22-65; T Boylston)

Wally's Café   JAZZ

15 ⭐ Map p80, A4

When Wally's opened in 1947, Barbadian immigrant Joseph Walcott became the first African American to own a nightclub in New England. Old-school, gritty and small, it still attracts a racially diverse crowd to hear jammin' jazz music 365 days a year. Berklee students love this place, especially the nightly jam sessions (6pm to 9pm). (www.wallyscafe.com; 427 Massachusetts Ave; ⏰5pm-2am; T Massachusetts Ave)

Shopping

Bobby From Boston   VINTAGE

16 🔒 Map p80, E5

Bobby is one of Boston's coolest cats. Men from all over the greater Boston area come to the South End to peruse Bobby's amazing selection of classic clothing from another era. This is stuff that your grandfather wore – if he was a very stylish man. Smoking jackets, bow ties, bomber jackets and more. (www.bobby-from-boston.com; 19 Thayer St; ⏰noon-6pm Tue-Sun; 🚌SL4, SL5, T Tufts Medical Center)

Uniform   CLOTHING

17 🔒 Map p80, C4

With its cool collection of men's casual wear, Uniform caters to all the metrosexuals in this hipster 'hood. Guys leave this place decked out in designers like Ben Sherman and Penguin, with a Freitag bag slung over a shoulder. Looking good, gentlemen, looking good. (www.uniformboston.com; 511 Tremont St; ⏰11am-7pm Tue & Wed, to 8pm Thu-Sat, noon-5pm Sun; T Back Bay)

Sault New England

GIFTS & SOUVENIRS

18 🔒 Map p80, B4

Blending prepster and hipster, rustic and chic, this little basement boutique packs in a lot of intriguing stuff. The eclectic mix of merchandise runs the gamut from new and vintage clothing to coffee-table books and homemade terrariums. A New England theme runs through the store, with nods to the Kennedys, *Jaws* and LL Bean. (www.saultne.com; 577 Tremont St; ⏰10am-7pm Mon-Sat, to 5pm Sun; T Back Bay)

Explore

Back Bay

Back Bay includes the city's most fashionable window-shopping, latte-drinking and people-watching area, on Newbury St, as well as its most elegant architecture, around Copley Sq. Once an uninhabitable tidal flat (hence the name), the area was filled in to create a residential neighborhood of magnificent Victorian brownstones and high-minded civic plazas in the late 19th century.

The Sights in a Day

☼ Start your day with a coffee and scone from **Flour** (p98). Then walk a few blocks to Copley Sq, which offers the best of Back Bay architecture. Peek into **Trinity Church** (p92) to marvel at the stained-glass windows and multitiered murals. Then take a self-guided tour of the masterworks at the **Boston Public Library** (p90). Treat yourself to tea at the library's lovely restaurant **Courtyard** (p99).

☼ After admiring the architecture and browsing the books, you are perfectly placed for an afternoon of window-shopping and gallery-hopping along swanky Newbury St. Get a different perspective on the city at the **Prudential Center Skywalk Observatory** (p98) – or get a different perspective on the world at the **Mapparium** (p98).

☾ Take your pick from the neighborhood's fine venues for dinner, followed by live music at the **Red Room @ Café 939** (p101).

For a local's day in Back Bay, see p94.

👁 Top Sights

Boston Public Library (p90)

Trinity Church (p92)

🔍 Local Life

Back Bay Fashion Walk (p94)

❤ Best of Boston

Eating

Atlantic Fish Co (p99)

Flour (p98)

Courtyard (p99)

Drinking

Top of the Hub (p100)

Entertainment

Red Room @ Café 939 (p101)

Shopping

Lunarik Fashions (p95)

Ball & Buck (p95)

Getting There

T **Metro** Take the green line to Copley, Hynes or Prudential, or the orange line to Back Bay station.

Top Sights
Boston Public Library

Dating from 1852, the esteemed Boston Public Library (BPL) was built as a 'shrine of letters,' lending credence to Boston's reputation as the Athens of America. The old McKim building is notable for its magnificent facade (inspired by Italian Renaissance palazzi) and exquisite interior art. As you enter, note Mora and Saint-Gaudens' carving of Minerva, goddess of wisdom, on the central keystone on the facade. Then proceed through Daniel Chester French's monumental bronze doorways, flanked by iron gates and lanterns.

Map p96, E3

www.bpl.org

700 Boylston St

9am-9pm Mon-Thu, to 5pm Fri & Sat year-round, plus 1-5pm Sun Oct-May

T Copley

Puvis de Chavannes Gallery

The main marble staircase leads past Pierre Puvis de Chavannes' inspirational murals depicting poetry, philosophy, history and science, which he considered the four great expressions of the human mind. Upstairs, at the entrance to Bates Hall, is another Puvis de Chavannes mural, with the nine muses from Greek mythology honoring the Genius of the Enlightenment.

Bates Hall

The staircase terminates at Bates Hall Reading Room, where even mundane musings are elevated by the barrel-vaulted, 50ft coffered ceilings. In 1852 Joshua Bates was the BPL's original benefactor, stipulating that 'the building shall be...an ornament to the city, that there shall be a room for 100 to 150 persons to sit at reading tables, and that it shall be perfectly free to all.'

Abbey Room

The Abbey Room is among the library's most sumptuous, with its oak wainscoting, checkerboard marble floors, elaborate fireplace and coffered ceiling inspired by the Doge's Palace in Venice. The room is named for the painter of the 1895 murals, which recount Sir Galahad's Quest for the Holy Grail.

Sargent Gallery

On the 3rd floor is the library's pièce de résistance: John Singer Sargent's unfinished mural series, *The Triumph of Religion*. Sargent's paintings trace the history of Western religion, from paganism to Judaism to Christianity. A final mural was intended for the vacant space above the stairwell, but it was never completed, due in part to strong criticism from the Jewish community.

☑ Top Tips

▶ The BPL offers free guided art and architecture tours, leaving from the entrance hall at various times throughout the week; see the BPL website for a current schedule.

▶ The special collections hold countless treasures, including John Adams' personal library. Check the website for details of exhibits showcasing the highlights, as well as a schedule of free events, from author talks to musical performances.

▶ Don't leave without taking a moment of contemplation in the peaceful Italianate courtyard.

✗ Take a Break

Grab a coffee, sandwich or salad at the on-site **Map Room Cafe** (www.thecateredaffair.com; Boston Public Library; snacks, salads & sandwiches $5-11; ⏱9am-5pm Mon-Sat; 🛜✐).

For an exquisite afternoon tea, head next door to the more formal Courtyard (p99).

Top Sights
Trinity Church

A masterpiece of American architecture, Trinity Church is the country's ultimate example of Richardsonian Romanesque. The granite exterior, with a massive portico and side cloister, uses sandstone in colorful patterns. The interior is an awe-striking array of vibrant murals and stained glass, most by artist John LaFarge, who cooperated closely with architect Henry Hobson Richardson to create an integrated composition of shapes, colors and textures.

◉ Map p96, E3

www.trinitychurchboston.org

206 Clarendon St

tours adult/child $7/free

🕙 10am-5pm Tue-Sat, 1-5pm Sun Easter-Oct, reduced hours rest of year

T Copley

LaFarge Murals

The walls of the great central tower are covered by two tiers of murals, soaring more than 100ft high. Prior to this commission, LaFarge did not have experience with mural painting on this scale. The result – thousands of square feet of exquisite, jewel-toned encaustic paintings – established his authority as the father of the American mural movement.

Stained-Glass Windows

The 33 stained-glass windows – mostly executed by different glass workshops – represent diverse styles. The original windows from 1877 and 1878 are the traditional European designs, completed by premier English workshops. Several later examples represent the English arts-and-crafts movement, while the ornate French windows were designed by Parisian artist Achille François Oudinot.

LaFarge Windows

The jewels of the church are the work of LaFarge, distinctive for their use of layered opalescent glass, resulting in an unprecedented richness of shades and dimensions. LaFarge's first commission was *Christ in Majesty*, the spectacular three-panel clerestory window at the western end that is now considered one of the USA's finest examples of stained-glass art.

Architecture

The footprint of Trinity Church is a Greek cross, with chancel, nave and transepts surrounding the central square. The wide-open interior was a radical departure from traditional Episcopal architecture, but it embodies the democratic spirit of the congregation in the 1870s.

☑ **Top Tips**

▶ Free architectural tours are offered following Sunday service at 11:15am. Additional tours are offered daily throughout the week (times vary).

▶ Free concerts on the impressive pipe organ are held on Fridays at 12:15pm.

▶ Snap a photo from Clarendon St to catch the exquisite church reflected in the facade of the nearby John Hancock Tower.

✖ **Take a Break**

Stop for sustenance at Flour (p98), which gets rave reviews for rich coffee, fresh-made scones and pastries, and delectable soups and sandwiches. For something more substantial, feast on crab cakes, chowder and lobster ravioli at Atlantic Fish Co (p99).

Local Life
Back Bay Fashion Walk

Welcome to designer row. On Newbury St, you'll have no problem procuring Diesel jeans, a Fendi bag or an Armani suit. But this is also the place to discover fashion with a distinctly Bostonian twist – from custom-made Converse sneakers to boutiques and galleries featuring local designers.

❶ School of Fashion Design
Up-and-coming local talents hone their skills and experiment with their ideas at the **School of Fashion Design** (www.schooloffashiondesign.org; 136 Newbury St; admission free; ⏱hours vary; Ⓣ Copley), Boston's only educational institution focusing exclusively on fashion. Check out the 'fashion artspace' at the on-site A Gallery, which hosts exhibits exploring the intersection of fashion, art and design.

❷ Ball & Buck

The hunter logo at **Ball & Buck** (📞617-262-1776; www.ballandbuck.com; 144b Newbury St; 🕙10am-8pm; Ⓣ Copley) is indicative of this brand's target market – manly men who look good in camouflage and love America. Both sophisticated and sporty, these attractive, durable duds are meant to be worn in the woods or on the Boston city streets. Made in the US.

❸ Daniela Corte

Born and raised in Buenos Aires, Daniela Corte attended the Boston School of Fashion Design before launching her own line and opening this sleek **boutique** (📞617-262-2100; www.danielacorte.com; 211 Newbury St, 2nd fl; 🕙by appointment Mon-Fri; Ⓣ Copley) on Newbury St. Browse her collection of silky tops, fun dresses and skin-hugging leggings, all of which are made in the upstairs studio.

❹ Lunarik Fashions

Like a modern woman's handbag, **Lunarik** (279 Newbury St; 🕙11am-7pm Mon-Fri, 10am-8pm Sat, noon-6pm Sun; Ⓣ Hynes) is packed with useful stuff, much of it by local designers. Look for whimsical collage-covered pieces by Jenn Sherr, beautiful hand-crafted jewelry by Dasken Designs, and the best-selling, richly colored leather handbags by Saya Cullinan.

❺ Three Wise Donkeys

Made-to-order T-shirts are the name of the game at this unique **shop** (www.facebook.com/ThreeWiseDonkeys; 51 Gloucester St; 🕙11am-6pm Mon-Thu, 11am-8pm Fri & Sat, noon-5pm Sun; Ⓣ Hynes Convention Center). Browse the artwork that lines the walls, find a design that you like and they'll print it on an organic cotton T-shirt in the color and style of your choosing – all in 15 minutes.

❻ Converse

Converse (www.converse.com; 348 Newbury St; 🕙10am-7pm Mon-Fri, to 8pm Sat, 11am-6pm Sun; Ⓣ Hynes) started making shoes right up the road in Malden, MA, way back in 1908. Chuck Taylor joined the 'team' in the 1920s and the rest is history. This retail store carries sneakers, denim and other gear. The iconic shoes come in all colors and patterns; better yet, make them uniquely your own at the 2nd-floor customization area.

A B C D

1

Harvard Bridge

Charles River

2A

Charles River Bike Path

Back St

Beacon St

Storrow Dr

Marlborough St

2

Storrow Dr

Massachusetts Ave

Charlesgate Overpass

Hereford St

Gloucester St

Fairfield St

Commonwealth Ave

2

BACK BAY

Exeter St

Kenmore

Newbury St

⊗ 4

3

90

Massachusetts Turnpike

Boylston St

⊗ 6

Ring Rd

Ipswich St

⊕ 14

✿ 10

Hynes Convention
🚇 Center

Hynes
Convention
Center

Prudential
◉ Center Skywalk
1 Observatory

8 ⊕

Scotia St

Dalton St

✿ 12

Belvidere St

Haviland St

St Germain St

🚇 Prudential

4

Community
Victory
Gardens

Muddy River

Norway St

Edgerly Rd

Mary Baker Eddy
2 ◉ Library &
Mapparium

FENWAY

Burbank St

Huntington Ave

St Botolph St

Westland Ave

Claremont St

Durham St

Agassiz Rd

Hemenway St

Symphony Rd

Symphony
Hall

Symphony St Stephens St

🚇 Symphony

Cumberland St

5

Kelleher
Rose
Garden

The Fenway

Gainsborough St

Columbus Ave

Massachusetts 🚇
Avenue

E F G H

Byron St

Beacon St

The
Esplanade

Public
Garden

Boston
Common

Storrow Dr

Arlington St

Charles St

28

Clarendon St

Berkeley St

Commonwealth Ave

The
Lagoon

2

Dartmouth St

2

Newbury St

5 ✗ T 7 ✗

Boylston St Boylston

Arlington

Four
Seasons
Hotel

T

Boylston St

Tremont St

2

Boylston St

Providence St Park Plaza

**THEATER
DISTRICT**

Stuart St

L3 Copley

T Copley
Square

St James Ave

Statler
Park

Tufts
Medical
Center

Trinity
Church

Boston
Public
Library

John
Hancock
Tower

Stuart St

Church St

Charles St S

T

Blagden St

Trinity Pl

✗ 3

9 ✗ Columbus Ave

Isabella St

Cortes St

Melrose St

Fayette St

Tremont St

3

Tremont St

Massachusetts Turnpike

Marginal Rd

CHINATOWN

Back Bay/
South End

Herald St

90

Tent
City

W Canton St

Yarmouth St

Lawrence St

Clarendon St

Chandler St

Berkeley St

Paul Pl

Tremont St

Shawmut Ave

Washington St

4

Appleton St

Gray St

Holyoke St

Dartmouth St

Warren Ave

**SOUTH
END**

Milford St

Hanson St

Columbus
Square

W Brookline St

Montgomery St

Upton St
Drapers La

For reviews see

◉ Top Sights   p90
◉ Sights   p98
✗ Eating   p98
🍷 Drinking   p100
✧ Entertainment   p101
🔒 Shopping   p103

W Newton St

Pembroke St

Rutland Sq

Tremont St

W Dedham St

Shawmut Ave

ROXBURY

N 0   400 m
   0   0.2 miles

5

Sights

Prudential Center Skywalk Observatory
VIEWPOINT

1 ◉ Map p96, D4

Technically called the Shops at Prudential Center, this landmark Boston building is not much more than a fancy shopping mall. But it does provide a bird's-eye view of Boston from its 50th-floor Skywalk. Completely enclosed by glass, the Skywalk offers spectacular 360-degree views of Boston and Cambridge, accompanied by an entertaining audiotour (with a special version catering to kids). Alternatively, enjoy the same view from Top of the Hub (p100) for the price of a drink. (www.skywalkboston.com; 800 Boylston St; adult/child $18/13; ⊙10am-10pm Mar-Oct, to 8pm Nov-Feb; P 👬; T Prudential)

Q Local Life
Charles River Esplanade

Perfect for picnic lunches and summertime lounging, this **riverside park** (www.esplanadeassociation.org; 👬; T Charles/MGH, Kenmore) is Boston's backyard. Designed by Frederick Law Olmsted, the Esplanade stretches almost 3 miles along the Boston shore of the Charles River, from the Museum of Science to Boston University Bridge. Paths along the river are ideal for bicycling, jogging or walking.

Mary Baker Eddy Library & Mapparium
LIBRARY

2 ◉ Map p96, C4

The Mary Baker Eddy Library houses one of Boston's hidden treasures. The intriguing Mapparium is a room-sized, stained-glass globe that visitors walk through on a glass bridge. It was created in 1935, which is reflected in the globe's geopolitical boundaries. The acoustics, which surprised even the designer, allow everyone in the room to hear even the tiniest whisper. (www.marybakereddylibrary.org; 200 Massachusetts Ave; adult/child $6/4; ⊙10am-4pm Tue-Sun; 👬; T Symphony)

Eating

Flour
BAKERY $

3 🍴 Map p96, F3

Joanne Chang's beloved bakery is taking over Boston. This outlet – on the edge of Back Bay – has the same flaky pastries and rich coffee that we have come to expect, not to mention sandwiches, soups, salads and pizzas. And just to prove there is something for everybody, Flour also sells homemade dog biscuits for your canine friend. (✆617-437-7700; www.flourbakery.com; 131 Clarendon St; pastries from $3, sandwiches $9; ⊙6:30am-8pm Mon-Fri, 8am-6pm Sat, 8am-5pm Sun; 🛜 🖊 👬; T Back Bay)

COURTESY OF THE MARY BAKER EDDY LIBRARY, BOSTON, MA

Mapparium, Mary Baker Eddy Library

Courtyard
AMERICAN $$$

The perfect destination for an elegant afternoon tea is – believe it or not – the Boston Public Library (see  Map 96, E3). Overlooking the beautiful Italianate courtyard, this grown-up restaurant serves an artfully prepared selection of sandwiches, scones and sweets, accompanied by a wide range of teas (black, green and herbal) and an optional glass of sparkling wine. Reserve ahead, especially on Saturdays. (☎617-859-2251; www.thecateredaffair.com/bpl; 700 Boylston St; tea adult/child $39/19, with sparkling wine $49; ☻11:30am-3pm Mon-Sat; Ⓣ Copley)

Atlantic Fish Co
SEAFOOD $$$

4 🍴 Map p96, D3

New England clam chowder in a bread bowl: for a perfect lunch here, that's all you need to know. For nonbelievers, we will add seafood *fra diavolo*, lobster ravioli and local Jonah crab cakes. There's more, of course, and the menu is printed daily to showcase the freshest ingredients. Enjoy it in the seafaring dining room or on the flower-filled sidewalk patio. (☎617-267-4000; www.atlanticfishco.com; 761 Boylston St; mains lunch $16-34, dinner $22-50; ☻11:30am-11pm; Ⓣ Copley)

Parish Café
SANDWICHES $

5 🍴 Map p96, F2

Sample the creations of Boston's most famous chefs without exhausting your expense account. The menu at Parish features a rotating roster of salads and sandwiches, each designed by local celebrity chefs, including Joanne Chang, Ken Oringer and Tony Maws. The place feels more 'pub' than 'cafe,' with a long bar backed by big TVs and mirrors. (☎617-247-4777; www.parishcafe.com; 361 Boylston St; sandwiches $12-20; ☻11:30am-1am, bar to 2am; ✎; Ⓣ Arlington)

L'Espalier
FRENCH $$$

6 🍴 Map p96, D3

This tried-and-true favorite remains the crème de la crème of Boston's culinary scene, thanks to impeccable service and a variety of prix-fixe and tasting menus. The offerings change daily, but usually include a degustation of caviar, a degustation of seasonal vegetables, and recommended wine pairings. (📞617-262-3023; www.lespalier.com; 774 Boylston St; lunch mains $31, prix-fixe dinner menus $98-118, degustation $208; ⏰11:30am-2:30pm & 5:30-9:30pm Sun-Thu, to 10:30pm Fri & Sat; 🚇Prudential)

Bistro du Midi
FRENCH $$

7 🍽️ Map p96, G2

The upstairs dining room is exquisite, but the downstairs cafe exudes warmth and camaraderie, inviting casual callers to linger over wine and snacks. In either setting, the Provençal fare is artfully presented and delicious. Reservations are required for dinner upstairs, but drop-ins are welcome at the cafe all day. (📞617-426-7878; www.bistrodumidi.com; 272 Boylston St; mains cafe $12-24, dining room $26-42; ⏰cafe 11:30am-10pm Mon-Fri, 3-10pm Sat & Sun, dining room 5-10pm; 🚇Arlington)

Drinking

Bukowski Tavern
BAR

8 🍺 Map p96, C3

This sweet bar lies inside a parking garage next to the canyon of the Mass Pike. Expect sticky wooden tables, loud rock music, lots of black hoodies, plenty of cussing, a dozen different burgers and dogs, and more than 100 kinds of beer. In God we trust; all others pay cash. (www.bukowskitavern.net; 50 Dalton St; ⏰11:30am-2am Mon-Sat, noon-2am Sun; 🚇Hynes)

Top of the Hub
BAR

Yes, it's touristy. And overpriced. And the food is not too inspiring. But the head-spinning city view makes it worthwhile to ride the elevator up to the 52nd floor of the Prudential Center (see 1 🔵 Map96, D4). Come for spectacular sunset drinks and stay for free live jazz. Beware the $24 per-person minimum after 8pm. (📞617-536-1775; www.topofthehub.net; 800 Boylston St; ⏰11:30am-1am; 🛜; 🚇Prudential)

Club Café
GAY

9 🍺 Map p96, F3

It's a club! It's a cafe! It's cabaret! Anything goes at this glossy, gay nightlife extravaganza. There is live cabaret in the Napoleon Room six nights a week, while the main dance and lounge area has tea parties, salsa dancing, trivia competitions, karaoke, bingo and good old-fashioned dance parties. (www.clubcafe.com; 209 Columbus Ave; ☺11am-2am; T Back Bay)

Entertainment

Red Room @ Café 939   LIVE MUSIC

10 ⭐ Map p96, C3

Run by Berklee students, the Red Room @ 939 has emerged as one of Boston's least predictable and most enjoyable music venues. It has an excellent sound system and a baby grand piano; most importantly, it books interesting, eclectic up-and-coming musicians. Buy tickets in advance at the Berklee Performance Center (p101). (www.cafe939.com; 939 Boylston St; T Hynes)

Hatch Memorial Shell   CONCERT VENUE

11 ⭐ Map p96, F1

Free summer concerts take place at this outdoor bandstand on the banks of the Charles River. Most famously, there's Boston's biggest annual music event, the Boston Pops' July 4 concert. But throughout the summer, there are also Friday-night movies, Wednesday-night orchestral ensembles and the occasional oldies concert. (www.hatchshell.com; Charles River Esplanade; T Charles/MGH, Arlington)

Berklee Performance Center

BLUES, JAZZ

12 ⭐ Map p96, C4

The performance hall at this notable music college hosts a wide variety of performances, from high-energy jazz recitals and songs by smoky-throated vocalists to oddball sets by keyboard-tapping guys who look like their day job is dungeon master. (www.berklee.edu/bpc; 136 Massachusetts Ave; tickets $8-58; T Hynes)

Understand
Weather or Not

- - - - - - - - - - - - - - -

Steady blue, clear view;
Flashing blue, clouds
are due;
Steady red, rain ahead;
Flashing red, snow instead.

Since 1950, Bostonians have used this simple rhyme and the weather beacon atop the old Hancock tower (next to the new John Hancock Tower) to determine if they need to take their umbrella when they leave the house. And yes, the beacon has been known to flash red in midsummer, but that is not a warning of some extremely inclement New England weather, but rather an indication that the Red Sox game has been canceled for the night.

Understand

Boston Marathon

Patriots' Day – officially celebrated on the third Monday in April – means more than Paul Revere's ride and 'the shot heard round the world'. Since 1897, Patriots' Day has also meant the **Boston Marathon** (www.baa.org; ⊘3rd Mon Apr). Fifteen people ran that first race (only 10 finished); in 2014 a record-breaking 35,755 people were registered to run.

Route

The 26-mile race starts in rural Hopkinton, MA, and winds its way through the western suburbs to Boston. Some of the marathon's most dramatic moments occur between mile 20 and 21, where the aptly named Heartbreak Hill rises a steep 80ft. It's all downhill from there.

Runners cruise up Beacon St, through Kenmore Sq, down 'Comm Ave' (Commonwealth Ave), over to Boylston St and into a triumphant finish at Copley Sq. This final mile is among the most exciting places to be a spectator.

Marathon Celebrities

The most infamous participant (loosely defined) is Rosie Ruiz, who in 1980 seemingly emerged from nowhere to win the women's division. In fact, she did emerge from nowhere, and had actually skipped most of the race. She was disqualified, but remains a Boston Marathon legend.

Modern marathon celebrities include Rick and Dick Hoyt (www. teamhoyt.com), a father-son team. Rick suffers from cerebral palsy, but his father was determined to give his son the chance to pursue his passions, including sports. With Dick pushing his son in a wheelchair, they have completed the Boston Marathon 32 times.

Marathon Bombings

In 2013 the nation (and the world) turned their eyes to Boston when two bombs exploded near the finish line of the Boston Marathon, killing three and injuring hundreds. Several days later, a Massachusetts Institute of Technology (MIT) police officer was shot dead and the entire city was locked down, as Boston became a battleground for the 'War on Terror.' The tragedy was devastating, but Boston claimed countless heroes, especially the many victims who inspired others with their courage and fortitude throughout their recoveries.

ANDREW BURTON/GETTY IMAGES ©

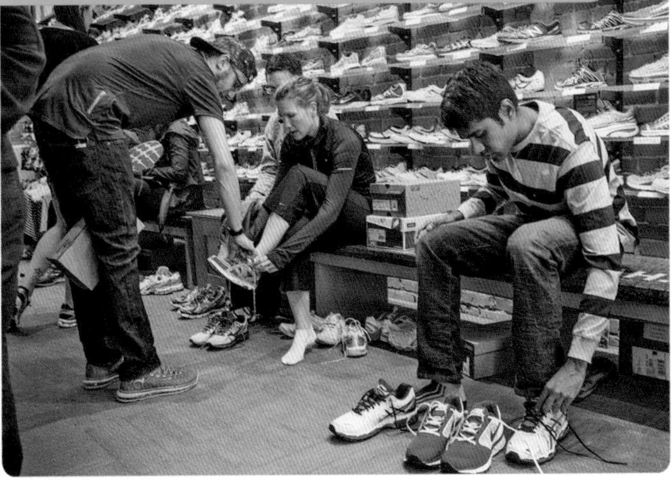

Marathon Sports

Shopping

Marathon Sports SPORTS & OUTDOORS

13 Map p96, E3

Specializing in running gear, this place could not have a better location: it overlooks the finish line of the Boston Marathon. It's known for attentive customer service, as staff work hard to make sure you get a shoe that fits. They also work hard to support the running community, with a weekly running club and a calendar of other events. (www.marathonsports.com; 671 Boylston St; 10am-7:30pm Mon-Wed & Fri, to 8pm Thu & Sat, 11am-6pm Sun; T Copley)

Newbury Comics MUSIC

14 Map p96, C3

How does a music store remain relevant in the digital world? One word: vinyl. In addition to the many cheap CDs and DVDs, there's a solid selection of new-release vinyl. Incidentally, it does sell comic books, as well as action figures and other silly gags. No wonder everyone is having such a wicked good time. (www.newburycomics.com; 332 Newbury St; 10am-10pm Mon-Sat, 11am-8pm Sun; T Hynes)

Explore

Kenmore Square & Fenway

Kenmore Square and Fenway are home to Boston's most beloved cultural institutions. The neighborhoods attract clubgoers and baseball fans to the streets surrounding Fenway Park, as well as art lovers and culture vultures to the artistic institutions along the Avenue of the Arts (Huntington Ave).

The Sights in a Day

☀ Decisions, decisions. You'll want to spend at least part of your day admiring the world-class artwork here in the Fenway, but you're going to have to decide which museum to patronize. It's easy to spend the entire day browsing in at the **Museum of Fine Arts** (p106), perusing the Art of the Americas wing, the impressionist and post-impressionist paintings and the ancient art. Or, you can spend a few hours in a more intimate art setting, studying the Italian Renaissance and Dutch Golden Age paintings at the **Isabella Stewart Gardner Museum** (p108).

☀ 'Mrs Jack' Gardner was a Red Sox fan – if you are too, head over to **Fenway Park** (p110) for a tour of America's oldest ballpark.

☾ You have another tough choice for the evening. Plan ahead to get tickets to hear the **Boston Symphony Orchestra** (p115) or to see the Red Sox play at home. Otherwise, indulge in dinner at **Island Creek Oyster Bar** (p113), followed by drinks at the **Hawthorne** (p115).

⦿ Top Sights

Museum of Fine Arts (p106)

Isabella Stewart Gardner Museum (p108)

Fenway Park (p110)

♥ Best of Boston

Eating
El Pelon (p113)

Island Creek Oyster Bar (p113)

Drinking
Bleacher Bar (p114)

Entertainment
Boston Symphony Orchestra (p115)

House of Blues (p115)

Huntington Theatre Company (p115)

Getting There

🇹 **Metro** To reach Kenmore Sq or Fenway Park, take any of the green-line trains except the E-line to Kenmore T station. For the Museum of Fine Arts, Boston Symphony Orchestra and other sights along Huntington Ave, take the green line's E train, or alternatively, the orange line to Mass Ave or Ruggles station.

Top Sights
Museum of Fine Arts

Since 1876, the Museum of Fine Arts has been Boston's premier venue for showcasing art by local, national and international artists. The museum's holdings are truly encyclopedic in scope, spanning the globe and encompassing all eras, from the ancient world to contemporary times. Most recently, the museum has added gorgeous new wings dedicated to the Art of the Americas and to contemporary art, contributing to Boston's emergence as an art center in the 21st century.

◉ Map p112, C4

www.mfa.org

465 Huntington Ave

adult/child $25/free weekends and after 3pm on weekdays

⊙ 10am-5pm Sat-Tue, to 10pm Wed-Fri

T Museum of Fine Arts; Ruggles

Art of the Americas

The centerpiece of the MFA is the four-story Americas wing. On the 2nd level is an entire gallery dedicated to John Singer Sargent, including his iconic painting *The Daughters of Edward Darley Boit*. Highlights in the American Impressionism galleries include pieces by Mary Cassat and perennial local favorite *At Dusk* by Childe Hassam.

Twentieth-Century European Art

The highlights of the European exhibit are the impressionist and post-impressionist galleries, with masterpieces by Degas, Gauguin, Renoir and Van Gogh, and an extensive collection of Monets (one of the largest outside Paris).

Buddhist Temple

Dimly lit and decorated with Buddhist statues, this room is a serene place to regroup before investigating the extensive collection of Asian art.

Egyptian Galleries

In the first half of the 20th century, the MFA and Harvard University cooperated to excavate tombs and temples surrounding the Giza Pyramids, bringing back thousands of artifacts that are now on display. Look for two rooms of mummies, as well as intriguing pottery and statuary.

Linde Family Wing for Contemporary Art

The recently renovated west wing – originally designed by IM Pei – has nearly tripled the exhibition space for contemporary art, with galleries dedicated to video, multimedia art and decorative arts. The darling of museum patrons is *Black River*, a fantastic woven tapestry of discarded bottle caps, by Ghanaian artist El Anatsui.

☑ Top Tips

▶ You can rent a guided multimedia tour (adult/child $6/4) in one of 10 languages, which uses video, audio and animation to provide extra insight on the museum's highlights.

▶ Children under the age of 17 are admitted free after 3pm on weekdays and all day on weekends.

▶ Before jumping into the collections, stop to admire the murals in the rotunda and above the main staircase, all painted by John Singer Sargent.

✖ Take a Break

The Linde Wing features upscale dining at **Bravo** (Mains $21-31; ⏱11:30am-3pm daily, 5:30-8:30pm Wed-Fri). In the Shapiro Courtyard, sample modern American cuisine at the **New American Café** (Sandwiches $16-18, mains $17-26; ⏱11:30am-4pm Sat-Tue, to 8pm Wed-Fri).

Top Sights
Isabella Stewart Gardner Museum

The magnificent Venetian-style palazzo that houses this museum was home to 'Mrs Jack' Gardner herself until her death in 1924. A monument to one woman's taste for acquiring exquisite art, the Gardner is filled with some 2500 priceless objects, primarily European, including tapestries, works from the Italian Renaissance and 17th-century Dutch paintings. The four-story greenhouse courtyard is a masterpiece and a tranquil oasis that alone is worth the price of admission.

👁 Map p112, C4

www.gardnermuseum.org

25 Evans Way

adult/child $15/free

🕐 11am-5pm Wed-Mon, to 9pm Thu

Ⓣ Museum of Fine Arts

Tapestry Room

Titian's Europa

The centerpiece of the 2nd-floor Titian room, this erotic painting was one of Mrs Gardner's favorites. As the story goes, the Roman god Jupiter disguised himself as a gentle white bull to seduce the princess Europa. He succeeded, and their offspring was supposedly the founder of Europe.

John Singer Sargent

Mrs Gardner was a patron of John Singer Sargent, who often used the palazzo as a studio. In the 1st-floor Spanish Cloister, the dramatic painting of a flamenco dancer, *El Jaleo*, is framed by a Moorish arch specifically designed for this space. Upstairs, the Gothic Room contains Sargent's stunning (and rather controversial) portrait of Mrs Gardner herself.

Tapestry Room

The majestic Tapestry Room evokes a castle hall, hung with 10 allegorical tapestries depicting scenes from the lives of Abraham and Cyrus the Great. The tapestries are hung haphazardly, rather than sequentially, according to Mrs Gardner's whim.

Empty Frames

On March 18, 1990, two thieves disguised as police officers broke into the Gardner and left with nearly $200 million worth of artwork, including paintings by Vermeer, Rembrandt, Manet and Degas, not to mention French and Chinese artifacts. The crime was never solved, and the frames still hang empty, to honor Mrs Gardner's request that her collection never be altered.

☑ Top Tips

▶ Admission to the Gardner is free on your birthday! If your name is Isabella, admission is free every day.

▶ Free tours and public talks are offered nearly every day, including an hour-long Collection Highlights Tour (at noon and 2pm on weekdays).

▶ Decked with ancient art and seasonal blooms, the courtyard is glorious from any angle. Check it out from the upper-story windows.

✘ Take a Break

If there isn't a free table at the elegant **Café G** (Isabella Stewart Gardner Museum; mains $16-19; ⏱11am-4pm Wed & Fri-Mon, 11am-8pm Thu) on the museum's ground floor, you'll receive a pager so you can explore the palazzo until your table is ready. Alternatively, exit the museum and stroll across the Back Bay Fens for a quick but satisfying lunch at El Pelon (p113).

Top Sights
Fenway Park

What is it that makes Fenway Park 'America's Most Beloved Ballpark'? It's not just that it's the home of the Boston Red Sox. Open since 1912, it's the oldest operating baseball park in the country. To learn its history and find out what's so special about Fenway, take the hour-long tour of this beloved Boston landmark. Bonus: see the ballpark from atop the legendary Green Monster!

👁 Map p112, C2

www.redsox.com

4 Yawkey Way

tours adult/child $20/14, premium tour $35

⊙9am-5pm

T Kenmore

Green Monster

As all Red Sox fans know, 'the wall giveth and the wall taketh away.' The 37ft-high left-field wall is only 310ft away from home plate (compared to the standard 325ft), so it's popular among right-handed hitters, who can score an easy home run with a high hit to left. However, batters can just as easily be deprived of a home run when a powerful – but excessively low – line drive bounces off the Monster for an off-the-wall double.

Scoreboard

At the base of the Green Monster is the original scoreboard, still updated manually from behind the wall.

Pesky Pole

The Pesky Pole, Fenway's right-field foul pole, is named for former shortstop Johnny Pesky. Johnny 'Mr Red Sox' Pesky was associated with the team for 15 years as a player and 46 as a manager, coach and special instructor.

The Triangle

Many a double has turned into a triple when the ball has flown into the deepest, darkest corner of center field (where the walls form a triangle). At 425ft, it's the furthest distance from home plate.

Red Seat

The bleachers at Fenway Park are green, except for one lone red seat: seat 21 at section 42, row 37. This is supposedly the longest home run ever hit at Fenway Park – officially 502ft, hit by Red Sox left fielder Ted Williams in 1946.

☑ **Top Tips**

▶ Tours depart at the top of the hour. Buy tickets online or at the Gate D ticket booth.

▶ If you want to see a game, it's best to buy tickets well in advance. Game-day tickets go on sale (one per person) at Gate E, 90 minutes before the game, but people start lining up well before that.

▶ On game days, you can watch the teams warm up if you join a special 'pre-game tour' ($35).

✕ **Take a Break**

Concessions line the ballpark's breezeway, selling hot dogs, nachos, pretzels and beer.

Outside the ballpark, you'll find food and drink at the Bleacher Bar (p114) or any of the joints along Lansdowne St.

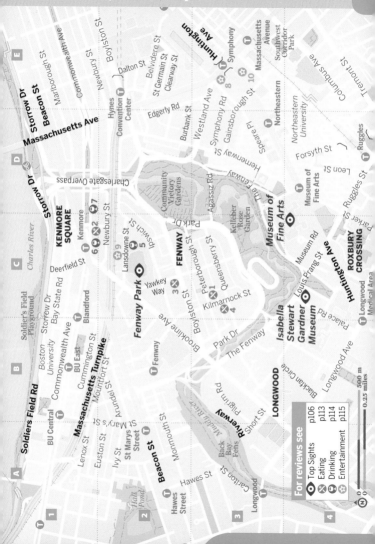

Massachusetts Avenue

Southwest
Corridor
Park

Huntington Ave

Symphony T

Belvidere St
St Germain St
Cleanway St

Massachusetts Ave T

8

10

Dalton St

Newbury St

Boylston St

Marlborough Ave

Commonwealth Ave

Marlborough St

Beacon St

Storrow Dr

Northeastern T

Northeastern
University

Forsyth St

Ruggles T

Leon St

Edgerly Rd

Burbank St

Westland Ave

Symphony Rd

Gainsborough St

Speare Pl

Columbus Ave

Tremont St

Hynes
Convention
Center T

Massachusetts Ave

Charlesgate Overpass

Storrow Dr

Charles River

KENMORE
SQUARE

Kenmore T

6 2 7

Deerfield St

Community
Victory
Gardens

Agassiz Rd

Hemenway St

The Fenway

Kelleher
Rose
Garden

Museum of
Fine Arts T

Museum of
Fine Arts

Parker St

Ruggles St

ROXBURY
CROSSING

Huntington Ave

Longwood
Medical Area

Longwood T

Newbury St

Lansdowne St

Ipswich St

9

FENWAY

5

Fenway Park

Yawkey
Way

3

Boylston St

Peterborough St

Queensberry St

Kilmarnock St

1

4

Museum Rd

Louis Prang St

Isabella
Stewart
Gardner
Museum

Palace Rd

Museum Rd

Boston
University

Commonwealth Ave

BU East T

Cummington St

Mountfort St

Blandford T

Bay State Rd

Storrow Dr

BU Central T

Soldiers Field Rd

Lenox St

Euston St

Ivy St

Arundel St

St Mary's St

St Marys
Street T

Brookline Ave

Park Dr

Fenway T

Park Dr

The Fenway

LONGWOOD

Brookline Ave

Blackfan Circle

Longwood Ave

Longwood T

Muddy River

Riverway

Pilgrim Rd

Short St

Back
Bay
Fens

Monmouth St

Hawes St

Hawes
Street T

Carlton St

Longwood T

Hall Pond

Beacon St

For reviews see
◇ Top Sights   p106
⊗ Eating   p113
🄳🄷 Drinking   p114
🄴 Entertainment   p115

500 m
0.25 miles

N

Clam chowder, Island Creek Oyster Bar

Eating

El Pelon
MEXICAN $

1 Map p112, C3

If your budget is tight, don't miss this chance to fill up on Boston's best burritos, tacos and tortas, made with the freshest ingredients. The *tacos de la casa* are highly recommended, especially the *pescado,* made with Icelandic cod and topped with chili mayo. Plates are paper and cutlery is plastic. (www.elpelon.com; 92 Peterborough St; tacos $4, burritos $6-8; ⊘11am-11pm; ⊿; ⊤Fenway)

Island Creek Oyster Bar
SEAFOOD $$$

2 Map p112, C1

Island Creek claims to unite farmer, chef and diner in one space – and what a space it is. ICOB serves up the region's finest oysters, along with other local seafood, in an ethereal new-age setting. The specialty – lobster-roe noodles topped with braised short ribs and grilled lobster – lives up to the hype. (☎617-532-5300; www.islandcreekoysterbar.com; 500 Commonwealth Ave; oysters $2.50-3.50, mains lunch $12-27, dinner $17-36; ⊘4-11pm Mon-Fri, 11:30am-11:30pm Sat, 10:30am-11pm Sun; ⊤Kenmore)

Understand
Citgo Sign

London has Big Ben, Paris has the Eiffel Tower and Boston has the Citgo sign. It's an unlikely landmark in this high-minded city, but Bostonians love the bright-blinking 'trimark' that has towered over Kenmore Sq since 1965. Every time the Red Sox hit a home run over the left-field wall at Fenway Park, Citgo's colorful logo is seen by thousands of fans. It also symbolizes the end of the Boston Marathon, as it falls at mile 25 in the race.

When Citgo decided to dismantle the deteriorating sign in the 1980s, local residents rallied to grant it landmark status, arguing it was a prime example of urban neon art. And the sign stayed. In 2005 the neon lights were replaced with LEDs (more durable, more energy efficient and easier to maintain). Featured in film, photos and song, the sign continues to shine.

Tasty Burger
BURGERS $

 3 Map p112, C2

Once a Mobil gas station, this place is now a retro burger joint, with picnic tables outside and a pool table inside. The name of the place is a nod to *Pulp Fiction,* as is the wall-mounted poster of Samuel L Jackson, whose character would surely agree that 'this is a tasty burger'. (www.tastyburger.com; 1301 Boylston St; burgers $5-6; ⏱11am-2am; T Fenway)

Tapestry
PIZZA $$

4 Map p112, C3

A Fenway newcomer, Tapestry is a dual-concept restaurant. In the Expo Kitchen, the chefs toss pizzas and shuck oysters in a sharp but casual setting. The adjacent Club Room is a higher-end lounge where guests sample innovative New American dishes – many of which may require looking up at least one ingredient. On weekends, brunch is served on the front patio. (www.tapestry.restaurant; 69 Kilmarnock St; mains brunch $10-17, dinner $14-23, pizzas $14-17; ⏱5:30-10pm Tue-Thu & Sun, to 11pm Fri & Sat, plus 10:30am-2:30pm Sat & Sun; T Museum of Fine Arts; Kenmore)

Drinking

Bleacher Bar
SPORTS BAR

5 Map p112, C2

Tucked under the bleachers at Fenway Park, this classy bar offers a view onto center field. It's not the best place to watch the game, as the place gets packed, but it's a fun way to experience America's oldest ballpark, even when the Sox are not playing. Gentlemen: enjoy the view from the loo! (www.bleacherbarboston.com; 82a Lansdowne St; ⏱11am-2am; T Kenmore)

Hawthorne
COCKTAIL BAR

6 🚇 Map p112, C1

Located in the basement of the Hotel Commonwealth, this is a living-room-style cocktail lounge that attracts the city's sophisticates. Sink into the plush furniture and sip a custom cocktail. (www.thehawthornebar.com; 500a Commonwealth Ave; ⏱5pm-1am; Ⓣ Kenmore)

Lower Depths Tap Room
BAR

7 🚇 Map p112, D1

This subterranean space is a beer-lovers' paradise, with all the atmosphere (and beer knowledge) of its sister establishment, Bukowski Tavern (p100). Besides the impressive beer selection, the kitchen – under the direction of beloved Boston chef Brian Poe – turns out a tasty array of tacos. Cash only. (www.thelowerdepths.com; 476 Commonwealth Ave; ⏱11:30am-1am; Ⓣ Kenmore)

Entertainment

Boston Symphony Orchestra
CLASSICAL MUSIC

8 ⭐ Map p112, E3

Flawless acoustics match the ambitious programs of the world-renowned Boston Symphony Orchestra. From September to April, the BSO performs in the beauteous **Symphony Hall** (301 Massachusetts Ave; ⏱hrs vary), featuring an ornamental high-relief ceiling and attracting a fancy-dress crowd. In summer months the BSO retreats to Tanglewood in Western Massachusetts. (BSO; ☎617-266-1200; www.bso.org; 301 Massachusetts Ave; tickets $30-145; Ⓣ Symphony)

House of Blues
LIVE MUSIC

9 ⭐ Map p112, C2

The HOB is bigger and better than ever. Well, it's bigger. Never mind the ridiculously tight security measures, this is where national acts play if they can't fill the Garden (eg the Bosstones, Dropkick Murphys etc). The balcony seating offers an excellent view of the stage, while fighting the crowds on the mezzanine can be brutal. (www.hob.com/boston; 15 Lansdowne St; Ⓣ Kenmore)

Huntington Theatre Company
THEATER

10 ⭐ Map p112, E3

Boston's leading theater company, the award-winning Huntington, specializes in developing new plays, staging many shows before they're transferred to Broadway (several of which have won Tony Awards). Seven major works by August Wilson were performed by the Huntington before going on to fame in New York. The company's credentials also include over 50 world premieres of works by playwrights such as Tom Stoppard and Christopher Durang. (Boston University Theatre; www.huntingtontheatre.org; 264 Huntington Ave; Ⓣ Symphony)

Explore

Cambridge

Stretched out along the north shore of the Charles River, Cambridge is a separate city that boasts two distinguished universities (Harvard and Massachusetts Institute of Technology, or MIT), a host of historic sites, and artistic and cultural attractions galore. The streets around Harvard Sq and Central Sq are home to restaurants, bars and clubs that rival their counterparts across the river.

The Sights in a Day

☀ First things first: take a tour of Harvard University's historic **Harvard Yard** (p118), then visit one of the university's top-notch museums, such as the **Peabody Museum of Archaeology & Ethnology** (p123) or the **Harvard Art Museums** (p123).

☀ Afterwards, have lunch at **Mr Bartley's Burger Cottage** (p125) or **Clover Food Lab** (p124). Spend the afternoon strolling along Tory Row, popping into **Longfellow House** (p124) and wandering around **Mt Auburn Cemetery** (p124).

☾ When you next get hungry, head to **Cambridge, 1** (p125) or **Alden & Harlow** (p125) for dinner. In the evening your options are nearly unlimited for cultural fare, whether it's live music, comedy, theater or film.

For a local's day in Harvard Square, see p120.

Top Sight

◉ Harvard Yard (p118)

○ Local Life

Offbeat Harvard Square (p120)

♥ Best of Boston

Eating

Clover Food Lab (p124)

Life Alive (p124)

Mr Bartley's Burger Cottage (p125)

Entertainment

American Repertory Theater (p127)

Comedy Studio (p126)

Sinclair (p127)

Museums

Harvard Art Museums (p123)

Getting There

🇹 **Metro** Take the red line to Harvard, Central or Kendall/MIT.

Top Sights
Harvard Yard

Founded in 1636 to educate men for the ministry, Harvard is America's oldest college. The original Ivy League school has eight graduates who went on to be US presidents, not to mention dozens of Nobel laureates and Pulitzer Prize winners. The geographic heart of Harvard University – where redbrick buildings and leaf-covered paths exude academia – is Harvard Yard.

◉ Map p122, B3

www.harvard.edu

Massachusetts Ave

tours free

T Harvard

Massachusetts Hall & Harvard Hall

Flanking Johnston Gate are the two oldest buildings on campus. South of the gate, Massachusetts Hall houses the offices of the president of the university. Dating to 1720, it is the oldest building at Harvard and the oldest academic building in the country. North is Harvard Hall, which dates to 1766 and originally housed the library.

John Harvard Statue

Every Harvard hopeful touches this statue's shiny shoe for good luck. Inscribed 'John Harvard, Founder of Harvard College, 1638,' it's been nicknamed the statue of three lies: it does not actually depict Harvard, but a random student; John Harvard was not the founder of the college, but its first benefactor; and the college was actually founded in 1636.

Widener Library

Behind this mass of Corinthian columns and steep stairs are more than 5 miles of books. Widener was built in memory of rare-book collector Harry Elkins Widener, who perished on the *Titanic*. A popular legend says that Harry gave up his seat in a lifeboat to retrieve his favorite book from his stateroom. The library is not open to the public.

Memorial Hall

North of Harvard Yard, just outside Bradstreet Gates and across the Plaza, this massive Victorian Gothic building was built to honor Harvard's Civil War heroes. The impressive Memorial Transept is usually open for visitors to admire the stained-glass windows and stenciled walls. Most of the building's artistic treasures are contained in Annenburg Hall, which is not open to the public.

☑ Top Tips

▸ Free student-led historical tours depart from the Smith Campus Center throughout the year.

▸ To go it alone, pick up a self-guided tour booklet (available in nine languages from the Smith Campus Center) or download an audio file or mobile app from the website.

▸ Finish your tour by climbing the steps of Robinson Hall for a perfectly framed photo of Memorial Hall.

✕ Take a Break

Harvard Sq is packed with places to eat and drink, including several spots near the Smith Campus Center. You can't go wrong at Clover Food Lab (p124) or Mr Bartley's Burger Cottage (p125).

Local Life
Offbeat Harvard Square

Overflowing with cafes, pubs, bookstores, record shops, street musicians and sidewalk artists, panhandlers and professors, Harvard Sq exudes energy and creativity. Tucked between the university and the river, the square and its neighboring streets still hold vestiges of Cambridge's traditional counterculture, if you know where to look.

1 The Pit

Start your tour in the center of Harvard Sq, where **Out of Town News** (⏱6am-10pm Sun-Thu, to 11pm Fri & Sat; **T**Harvard) has been selling international magazines and newspapers since 1955. The sunken area nearby, aka 'the Pit,' is popular with street artists, skateboarders and counterculture youth.

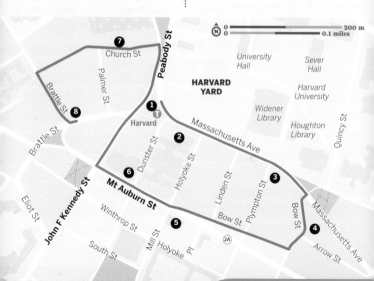

➋ Smith Campus Center

The sidewalk cafe in front of Harvard's main **administrative building** (www.harvard.edu/visitors; 30 Dunster St; ⏰9am-5pm Mon-Sat; Ⓣ Harvard) has hosted an ongoing chess tournament for 30 years and counting – look for the 'Play the Chessmaster' sign.

➌ Harvard Bookstore

The **Harvard Bookstore** (www.harvard. com; 1256 Massachusetts Ave; ⏰9am-11pm Mon-Sat, 10am-10pm Sun; Ⓣ Harvard) is not just a bookstore, but a reading community. Come in to browse the stacks and check out discounted 'seconds' in the basement. Next door, **Grolier Poetry Bookshop** (www.grolierpoetrybookshop.org; 6 Plympton St; ⏰11am-7pm Tue & Wed, to 6pm Thu-Sat; Ⓣ Harvard) is the oldest – and perhaps most famous – poetry bookstore in the US. Through the years, TS Eliot, EE Cummings, Marianne Moore and Allen Ginsberg have all passed through these doors.

➍ Cafe Pamplona

This perennially popular, no-frills European **cafe** (www.cafepamplona. weebly.com; 12 Bow St; ⏰11am-11pm; 🛜; Ⓣ Harvard) in a cozy backstreet cellar has been serving coffee and tea to Cantabrigian bohemians since 1959.

➎ In Your Ear

One of several excellent used-record shops in the square, **IYE** (www.iye.com; 72 Mt Auburn St; ⏰noon-8pm Mon-Sat, to 6pm Sun; Ⓣ Harvard) is located in the basement of a Harvard social club. It's totally disorganized, dusty and crammed with LPs and 45s, as well as CDs, DVDs and even eight-tracks.

➏ The Garage

This gritty **mini-mall** (36 John F Kennedy St; ⏰10am-10pm Mon-Sat, 11am to 8pm Sun; Ⓣ Harvard) (yes, formerly a parking garage) houses an eclectic mix of upstairs shops and downstairs eateries. Chill out with ice cream at Ben & Jerry's, listen to tunes at Newbury Comics, or get some ink at Chameleon Tattoo & Body Piercing.

➐ Raven Used Books

This beloved **shop** (www.ravencambridge. com; 23 Church St; ⏰10am-9pm Mon-Sat, 11am-8pm Sun; Ⓣ Harvard) is one of the last used-books holdouts in Harvard Sq. Relocated to spiffy new digs in 2015, Raven specializes in scholarly titles, with hundreds of new arrivals each week.

➑ Brattle Square

A few steps from the historic **Brattle Theatre** (www.brattlefilm.org; 40 Brattle St; Ⓣ Harvard), this intersection is a main stage for street performers. Tracy Chapman played here in the 1980s and Amanda Palmer was a living statue here in the 1990s. Puppeteer Igor Fokin also put on shows here until his unexpected death in 1996. Look for the tiny memorial sculpture erected to honor him – and by extension, all street performers.

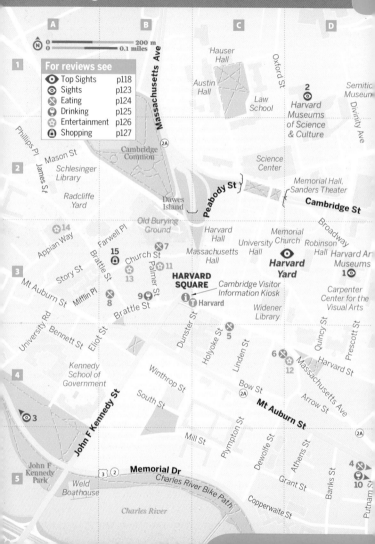

A | B | C | D

0 ——— 200 m
0 ——— 0.1 miles

For reviews see

◉ Top Sights   p118
◉ Sights   p123
✖ Eating   p124
🍷 Drinking   p125
🎭 Entertainment   p126
🛍 Shopping   p127

Hauser Hall

Austin Hall

Law School

Oxford St

Semitic Museum

2 ◎ Harvard Museums of Science & Culture

Divinity Ave

Massachusetts Ave

Phillips Pl

James St

Mason St

Schlesinger Library

Radcliffe Yard

Cambridge Common

Science Center

Memorial Hall, Sanders Theater

Peabody St

Dawes Island

Old Burying Ground

Cambridge St

14 ◎

Appian Way

Story St

Farwell Pl

Brattle St

15 🛍

Church St

13 ✖

Palmer St

7 ✖

11 ◎

Harvard Hall

Massachusetts Hall

University Hall

Memorial Church

Robinson Hall

Broadway

Harvard Yard ◉

Harvard Art Museums
1 ◎

Mt Auburn St

Mifflin Pl

Eliot St

8 ✖

9 🍷

Brattle St

HARVARD SQUARE

Cambridge Visitor Information Kiosk

ℹ ❶ Harvard

Widener Library

Carpenter Center for the Visual Arts

University Rd

Bennett St

Kennedy School of Government

Winthrop St

South St

Dunster St

Holyoke St

5 ✖

Linden St

Bow St

6 ✖

12

Quincy St

Prescott St

Harvard St

Massachusetts Ave

Arrow St

Mt Auburn St

3 ◎

John F Kennedy St

John F Kennedy Park

Weld Boathouse

3 2

Memorial Dr

Mill St

Plympton St

Dewolfe St

Athens St

Grant St

Banks St

Copperwaite St

Putnam Ave

4 ✖

10 🛍

Charles River Bike Path

Charles River

EVGENIAND/SHUTTERSTOCK ©

Harvard Museum of Natural History

Sights

Harvard Art Museums   MUSEUM

1 👁 Map p122, D3

The 2014 renovation and expansion
of Harvard's art museums allowed
the university's massive 250,000-piece
collection to come together under one
very stylish roof, designed by architect
extraordinaire Renzo Piano. The artwork spans the globe, with separate collections devoted to Asian and Islamic
cultures (formerly the Arthur M Sackler
Museum), northern European and
Germanic cultures (formerly the Busch-
Reisinger Museum) and other Western
art, especially European modernism
(formerly the Fogg). (www.harvardart

museums.org; 32 Quincy St; adult/child/stu-
dent $15/free/$10; ⊙10am-5pm; T Harvard)

Harvard Museums of Science & Culture   MUSEUM

2 👁 Map p122, D1

One ticket covers admission to both
esteemed science museums: the **Harvard Museum of Natural History** (www.
hmnh.harvard.edu; 26 Oxford St; 👶), with
the famed glass-flower exhibit, and
the **Peabody Museum of Archaeology
& Ethnology** (www.peabody.harvard.edu; 11
Divinity Ave), with its excellent collection
of artifacts from indigenous cultures.
(www.hmsc.harvard.edu; 11 Divinity Ave;
adult/child/senior $12/8/10; ⊙9am-5pm;
🚌86, T Harvard)

Understand

Tory Row

West of Harvard Sq, Brattle St is the epitome of colonial posh. Lined with mansions that were once home to royal sympathizers, the street earned the nickname Tory Row. Visit **Longfellow House** (📞617-876-4491; www.nps.gov/long; 105 Brattle St; admission free; ⊙tours 9:30am-5pm Wed-Sun late May-Oct, grounds dawn-dusk year-round; 🚌71, 73, 🚇Harvard), the stately Georgian mansion that once served as George Washington's headquarters and later home to epic poet Henry Wadsworth Longfellow. Continuing west, you'll discover tranquil Mt Auburn Cemetery, Longfellow's final resting place.

Mt Auburn Cemetery CEMETERY

3 ◎ Map p122, A4

This delightful spot at the end of Brattle St is worth the 30-minute walk west from Harvard Sq. Developed in 1831, it was the first 'garden cemetery' in the US. Maps pinpoint the rare botanical specimens and notable burial plots. Famous long-term residents include Mary Baker Eddy (founder of the Christian Science Church), Isabella Stewart Gardner (socialite and art collector), Winslow Homer (19th-century American painter), Oliver Wendell Holmes (US supreme court justice) and Henry

W Longfellow (19th-century writer). (www.mountauburn.org; 580 Mt Auburn St; admission free; ⊙8am-8pm May-Sep, to 5pm Oct-Apr; 🚌71, 73, 🚇Harvard)

Eating

Life Alive VEGETARIAN $

4 🍴 Map p122, D5

Life Alive offers a joyful, healthful, purposeful approach to fast food. The unusual combinations of animal-free ingredients yield delicious results, most of which come in a bowl (like a salad) or in a wrap. There are also soups, sides and smoothies, all served in a funky, colorful, light-filled space. (www.lifealive.com; 765 Massachusetts Ave; mains $6-10; ⊙8am-10pm Mon-Sat, 11am-7pm Sun; 🍴♿; 🚇Central)

Clover Food Lab VEGETARIAN $

5 🍴 Map p122, C4

Clover is on the cutting edge. It's all high-tech with its 'live' menu updates and electronic ordering system. But it's really about the food – local, seasonal, vegetarian fare – which is cheap, delicious and fast. How fast? Check the menu. Interesting tidbit: Clover started as a food truck (and still has trucks making the rounds). (www.cloverfoodlab.com; 1326 Massachusetts Ave; mains $8-11; ⊙7am-midnight Mon-Sat, 9am-10pm Sun; 📶🍴♿; 🚇Harvard)

Mr Bartley's Burger Cottage

BURGERS $

6 🍴 Map p122, C4

Packed with small tables and hungry college students, this burger joint has been a Harvard Sq institution for more than 50 years. Bartley's offers some 30 different burgers, including topical newcomers with names like Trump Tower and Tom Brady Triumphant; sweet-potato fries, onion rings, thick frappés and raspberry-lime rickeys complete the classic American meal. (www.mrbartley.com; 1246 Massachusetts Ave; burgers $7-16; ⏱11am-9pm Tue-Sat; T Harvard)

Cambridge, 1

PIZZA $$

7 🍴 Map p122, B3

This pizzeria is located in an old fire station – its name comes from the sign chiseled into the stonework out front. The interior is sleek, sparse and industrial, with big windows overlooking the Old Burying Ground in the back. The menu is equally simple: pizza, soup, salad, dessert. The oddly shaped pizzas are delectable, with crispy crusts and creative topping combos. (www.cambridge1.us; 27 Church St; pizzas $19-32; ⏱11:30am-midnight; 🍴; T Harvard)

Alden & Harlow

AMERICAN $$$

8 🍴 Map p122, B3

This subterranean space is offering a brand-new take on American cooking. The small plates are made for sharing, so everyone in your party gets to

sample the goodness. By the way, it's no secret that the 'Secret Burger' is amazing. Reservations are essential. Unfortunately, service suffers when the place get busy, which is often. (☎617-864-2100; www.aldenharlow.com; 40 Brattle St; small plates $15-18; ⏱10:30am-2pm Sat & Sun, 5pm-midnight Sun-Wed, 5pm-1am Thu-Sat; 🍴; T Harvard)

Drinking

Beat Brasserie

BAR

9 🍷 Map p122, B3

This vast, underground bistro packs in good-looking patrons for international food, classy cocktails and live jazz and blues. It's inspired by the Beat Generation writers – and named for a

---

🔍 Local Life
Food Trucks

Boston's thriving food truck culture started in Cambridge near Massachusetts Institute of Technology (MIT), where trucks catered to hungry students in search of cheap, filling fare. It's since grown to include additional hot spots such as Harvard Yard, the Boston Common and the Rose Kennedy Greenway. On summer weekends, don't miss the Food Truck Bazaar at the SoWa Open Market in Boston's South End. Learn more at the Boston Food Truck Blog (www.bostonfoodtruckblog.com) or Hub Food Trucks (www.hubfoodtrucks.com).

Understand

Massachusetts Institute of Technology (MIT)

The MIT campus offers a novel perspective on Cambridge academia: proudly nerdy, but not quite as tweedy as Harvard. Leave it to the mischievous brainiacs here to come up with the city's quirkiest museum – the **MIT Museum,** (http://mitmuseum.mit.edu; 265 Massachusetts Ave; adult/child $10/5; ⏱10am-6pm Jul & Aug, to 5pm Sep-Jun; P ♿; T Central) where you can meet humanoid robots or interact with the university's impressive collection of holograms. Guided tours of campus depart from the **MIT Information Center** (www.mit.edu; 77 Massachusetts Ave, No 7-121, Rogers Bldg; ⏱9am-5pm Mon-Fri; T Kendall/MIT).

---

run-down Parisian motel where they hung out – but there's nothing down-and-out about this hot spot. (www.beatbrasserie.com; 13 Brattle St; ⏱4pm-late Mon-Fri, 10am-late Sat & Sun; T Harvard)

Brick & Mortar   COCKTAIL BAR

10 🔲 Map p122, D5

Enter through the unmarked door (next to Central Kitchen) and climb the dark stairs to cool cocktail heaven. No pretenses here – just a pared-down setting and a choice list of craft cocktails and beers. The staff are knowledgeable and friendly, so if you don't see something you like, ask for advice. (www.brickmortarltd.com; 567 Massachusetts Ave; ⏱5pm-1am Sun-Wed, to 2am Thu-Sat; T Central)

Entertainment

Club Passim   LIVE MUSIC

11 ⭐ Map p122, B3

Folk music in Boston seems to be endangered outside of Irish bars, but

the legendary Club Passim does such a great job booking top-notch acts that it practically fills in the vacuum by itself. The colorful, intimate room is hidden off a side street in Harvard Sq, just as it has been since 1969. (✆617-492-7679; www.clubpassim.org; 47 Palmer St; tickets $10-32; T Harvard)

Comedy Studio   COMEDY

12 ⭐ Map p122, D4

The 3rd floor of the Hong Kong noodle house contains a low-budget comedy house with a reputation for hosting cutting-edge acts. This is where talented future stars (such as Brian Kiley, who became a writer for Conan O'Brien) refine their racy material. Each night has a different theme; on Tuesday, for instance, you can usually see a weird magic show. (www.thecomedystudio.com; 1238 Massachusetts Ave; shows $10-15; ⏱show 8pm Tue-Sun; T Harvard)

Longfellow House (p124)

American Repertory Theater
PERFORMING ARTS

14 ⭐ Map p122, A3

There isn't a bad seat in the house at the Loeb Drama Theater, where the prestigious ART stages new plays and experimental interpretations of classics. Artistic Director Diane Paulus encourages a broad interpretation of 'theater,' staging interactive murder mysteries, readings of novels in their entirety and robot operas. The ART's musical productions, in particular, have been racking up the Tonys. (ART; ☎617-547-8300; www.americanrepertorytheater.org; 64 Brattle St; tickets from $45; T Harvard)

Shopping

Cambridge Artists' Cooperative
ARTS & CRAFTS

15 🔒 Map p122, B3

Owned and operated by Cambridge artists, this two-level gallery displays an ever-changing exhibit of their work. The pieces are crafty: handmade jewelry, woven scarves, leather products and pottery. The craftspeople double as sales staff, so you may get to meet the creative force behind your souvenir. (www.cambridgeartistscoop.com; 59a Church St; ⏱10am-6pm Mon-Sat, 10am-7pm Thu, noon-6pm Sun; T Harvard)

Sinclair
LIVE MUSIC

13 ⭐ Map p122, B3

Top-notch small venue to hear live music. The acoustics are excellent and the mezzanine level allows you to escape the crowds on the floor. The club attracts a good range of local and regional bands and DJs. (www.sinclaircambridge.com; 52 Church St; tickets $15-35; ⏱5pm-1am Mon-Wed, 5pm-2am Thu & Fri, 11am-2am Sat, 11am-1am Sun; T Harvard)

The Best of
Boston

Boston's Best Walks

Freedom Trail. 130

Green Spaces
& Shopping Places 134

Boston's Best...

Eating. 136

Drinking. 138

Entertainment 140

Shopping. 141

For Kids 142

Museums 144

Spectator Sports 145

For Free. 146

History 147

Tours. 148

Boston's waterfront (p56)
ROMAN BABAKIN/SHUTTERSTOCK ©

Best Walks
Freedom Trail

🏃 The Walk

The best introduction to revolutionary Boston is the **Freedom Trail**, a redbrick path that winds its way past 16 sites that earned Boston its status as the 'cradle of American liberty.' The 2.4-mile trail follows the course of the conflict, from the Boston Common to Bunker Hill. Even though it's called the Freedom Trail, it covers much more than just revolutionary history – you'll find some of Boston's oldest landmarks, and sites where Boston prospered in the post-revolutionary period.

Start Boston Common: [T] Park St

Finish Bunker Hill Monument: [T] Community College

Length 2.4 miles; three to four hours

🍴 Take a Break

History buffs will appreciate **Union Oyster House** (p68), the oldest restaurant in the US, while vegetarians can recharge at **Clover Food Lab** (p66). **Quincy Market** (p68) food court offers myriad options for a quick lunch.

Massachusetts State House (p52)

❶ Boston Common

The Freedom Trail kicks off at the Boston Common (p46), America's oldest public park and the centerpiece of the city. The 50-acre green is crisscrossed with walking paths and dotted with monuments. Don't miss the monument to the victims of the Boston Massacre, erected in 1888.

❷ Massachusetts State House

Overlooking the Boston Common from the northeast corner, the Massachusetts State House (p52) occupies a proud spot atop the city's last remaining hill – land that was previously part of John Hancock's cow pasture. Other members of the Sons of Liberty (a clandestine network of patriots during the American Revolution) also had a hand in building the new capitol, literally: Samuel Adams and Paul Revere laid the cornerstones on July 4, 1795.

❸ Park St Church

Just south of the State House, the soaring spire

of Park St Church has been an unmistakable landmark since 1809. The church earned the moniker 'Brimstone Corner' both for its usage as a gunpowder storage place during the War of 1812 and for its fiery preaching.

❹ Granary Burying Ground

Walk north on Tremont St, where you will pass the Egyptian Revival gates of the Granary Burying Ground (p52). Steeped in history, the serene cemetery is the final resting place of many of the Sons of Liberty, as well as the victims of the Boston Massacre and other historical figures.

❺ King's Chapel & Burying Ground

Continue north to School St, where the Georgian King's Chapel (p64) overlooks its adjacent burying ground. It is perhaps an odd choice for inclusion on the Freedom Trail, since it was founded as an Anglican church in 1688. It does, however, contain a large bell crafted by Paul Revere,

and the prestigious Governor's pew, once occupied by George Washington.

❻ Site of the First Public School

Turn east on School St, and take note of

the bronze statue of Benjamin Franklin outside Old City Hall. A plaque commemorates this spot as the site of the country's first public school. Enter the courtyard to discover some of the

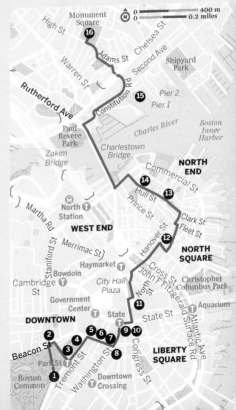

school's distinguished alumni and some quirky artwork.

❼ Old Corner Bookstore

Continue east to the intersection of School St and Washington St. The little brick building on your left is known as the Old Corner Bookstore, a literary hot spot for 75 years. Strangely, it is now a Mexican fast-food joint.

❽ Old South Meeting House

Diagonally opposite across Washington St, the Old South Meeting House (p64) saw the beginnings of one of the American Revolution's most vociferous protests, the Boston Tea Party. Come off the street and listen to a reenactment of what went down that day.

❾ Old State House

Before the revolution, the seat of the Massachusetts government was the Old State House (p64), a redbrick colonial edifice that is now surrounded by modern buildings and busy streets. Inside, you can peruse historic artifacts and listen to firsthand accounts of revolutionary events. Outside, gaze up at the balcony, where the Declaration of Independence was first read to Bostonians in 1776.

❿ Boston Massacre Site

In front of the Old State House, the cobblestone circle marks the site of the Boston Massacre (p48), the revolution's first violent conflict, in 1770. On March 5, an angry crowd of protesters was throwing snowballs and rocks at the British soldiers, who eventually fired into the crowd, killing five.

⓫ Faneuil Hall

Nearly every visitor to Boston stops at Quincy Market to grab a beer or shop for souvenirs, but most bypass historic Faneuil Hall (p65), the original market and public meeting place that was built in 1740. Pause to admire the bronze statue of Samuel Adams, who sits astride his horse in Dock Sq. Then ascend to the 2nd-floor hall, where Adams was one of the many orators to speak out against British rule.

⓬ Paul Revere House

From Faneuil Hall, cross the Rose Kennedy Greenway and head up Hanover St into the heart of the North End. A zigzag right onto Richmond St and left on North St brings you to charming North Sq, once home to Paul Revere. The weathered clapboard house here – Paul Revere House (p36) – is the oldest example in Boston, as most other wooden construction was destroyed by the fires that ravaged the city. This is likely where Paul Revere commenced his famous midnight ride.

⓭ Old North Church

Back on Hanover St, walk two blocks north to Paul Revere Mall. Besides a dramatic statue of the patriot himself, this park also provides a lovely vantage point to view your next destination, the Old North Church (p36). In addition to playing a crucial revolutionary

USS Constitution (p25)

role, the 1723 church is also Boston's oldest house of worship. Take a breather in the delightful gardens behind the church.

14 Copp's Hill Burying Ground

From the church, head west on Hull St to Copp's Hill Burying Ground (p36). This quiet corner contains some of the city's oldest gravestones and offers grand views across the river to Charlestown. See if you can find the headstone of Daniel Malcolm, which is littered with bullet holes from British troops who apparently took offense at his epitaph.

Incidentally, little is known about Malcolm's actual role in protests or revolution; historical records only show that he was arrested for failing to pay duty on 60 casks of wine.

15 USS Constitution

Continue west on Hull St to its end. Turn left on Commercial St and walk across the Charlestown Bridge. Turning right on Constitution Rd brings you to the Charlestown Navy Yard, home of the world's oldest commissioned warship, the USS Constitution (p25). Board the ship for a tour of the upper decks, where

you will learn about its exploits in America's earliest naval battles.

16 Bunker Hill Monument

Walk through the winding cobblestone streets up to the 220ft granite obelisk that is the Bunker Hill Monument (p27). Check out the dioramas in the museum to better understand what transpired on that fateful day in June 1775, when the Battle of Bunker Hill took place. Then climb 294 steps to the top of the monument to enjoy the panorama of the city, the harbor and the North Shore.

Best Walks
Green Spaces & Shopping Places

🏃 The Walk

Everybody knows about its world-class museums and historical sites, but Boston also offers a network of verdant parks, welcoming waterways and delightful shopping streets, making it a wonderful walking city. Take a break from the crowded downtown streets and discover another side of Boston.

Start Boston Common: **T** Park St

Finish Boston Common: **T** Park St

Length 2.5 miles; three hours

🍴 Take a Break

Fuel up ahead of time with coffee and pastries at **Flour** (p98) or **Wired Puppy** (www.wiredpuppy.com; 250 Newbury St; 🕧6:30am-7:30pm; 🛜; **T**Hynes), or wait till your walk's end and grab a meal at **Paramount** (p53).

Boston Common (p46)

❶ Boston Common

Welcome to the country's oldest public park (p46), sprinkled with monuments and memorabilia. Follow busy Bostonians crisscrossing the Common and exit the park from the western side.

❷ Public Garden

The Public Garden (p52) is a 24-acre botanical oasis of Victorian flowerbeds, verdant grass and weeping willows shading a tranquil lagoon. At any time of year, don't miss the famous statue *Make Way for Ducklings*, based on the beloved children's book.

❸ Newbury Street

Exiting the Public Garden through its southwestern gate, stroll west on swanky Newbury St, perfect for window-shopping and people-watching.

❹ Copley Square

Boston's most exquisite architecture is clustered around this stately Back Bay plaza. The Romanesque Trinity Church (p92) is particularly lovely as reflected in the modern John Hancock Tower. Opposite, the elegant neo-Renaissance Boston Public Library (p90) is packed with treasures.

5 Commonwealth Avenue

Heading north, cross stately Commonwealth Ave, the grandest of Back Bay's grand avenues. Lined with brownstones and studded with 19th-century art, the 'Mall' offers an eclectic perspective on history.

6 Charles River Esplanade

The southern bank of the Charles River Basin is known as the Esplanade (p98), an enticing urban escape with grassy knolls and cooling waterways designed by Frederick Law Olmsted. Walk northeast, enjoying the breezes and views of the river.

7 Charles Street

Intriguing history, iconic architecture and unparalleled neighborhood charm make Beacon Hill one of Boston's

most prestigious addresses. Traversing the flat of the hill, Charles St is an enchanting spot for browsing boutiques and haggling over antiques.

8 Louisburg Square

Stroll down residential streets lit with gas lanterns, admire the distinguished brick town houses, and discover streets such as stately Louisburg Sq (p53) that capture the neighborhood's grandeur. Continue south to return to the Common.

Best
Eating

The Boston area is the home of the first Thanksgiving and of bountiful autumnal harvests. It's also America's seafood capital, home to dishes such as clam chowder and boiled lobster. This regional cuisine has deep cultural roots – and like all things cultural, is dynamic and continuously developing.

PAT GREENHOUSE/THE BOSTON GLOBE VIA GETTY IMAGES ©

International Influences

The international influence on Boston cuisine cannot be underestimated. A tight-knit immigrant enclave, the North End is a bastion of old-fashioned Italian American cooking, with ristoranti, *enoteche* (wine bars) and *pasticcerie* (bakeries) around every corner.. In the 20th century, a new wave of immigrants arrived from South America and Asia, bringing the flavors of Brazil, China, India, Korea and Vietnam.

Farm to Table

In this era of creative culinary discovery, more and more Bostonians are reclaiming their roots in one crucial way: through their appreciation of local, seasonal and organic products. This thriving 'locavore' movement showcases the bounty of local waters and rich New England farms.

Vegetarians & Vegans

Boston boasts an ever-increasing number of vegetarian and vegan eateries. The Boston Vegetarian Society (www.bostonveg.org) is a great resource for vegetarians and vegans, and sponsors a fabulous two-day food festival in October.

☑ Top Tip

▶ In restaurants with sit-down service, customers should leave a 15% tip for acceptable service and a 20% tip for good service; anything less reflects dissatisfaction with the waiter. Waitstaff and bartenders are paid significantly below minimum wage and depend on tips for their earnings.

Best Location

Courtyard Inside the beautiful Boston Public Library. (p99)

Legal Harborside On the waterfront, with views of Boston Harbor. (p67)

Bistro du Midi Overlooking the Public Garden. (p100)

Clover Food Lab (p124)

Best Budget Eating

El Pelon Cheap and delicious tacos and other Mexican treats. (p113)

Galleria Umberto Lunch for less than $5. (p38)

Best Seafood

Neptune Oyster Casual but classy, with a well-stocked raw bar. (p37)

Yankee Lobster Co Retail fish market serving the freshest seafood around (p67)

Row 34 A dozen types of mollusks are served at this 'working man's oyster bar.' (p66)

Atlantic Fish Co All kinds of seafood, any way you like it. (p99)

Island Creek Oyster Bar Eat your seafood in style. (p113)

Best Italian

Coppa An authentic *enoteca* experience. (p82)

Pomodoro The quintessential North End hideaway. (p38)

Best Asian

Myers & Chang Pan-Asian delights. (p82)

Gourmet Dumpling House Ridiculously good soup dumplings. (p82)

Best Pizza

Pizzeria Regina The queen of pizza in Boston. (p38)

Cambridge, 1 Innovative toppings. (p125)

Best Vegetarian

Clover Food Lab Fast food, made fresh, with no animals involved. (p124)

Life Alive Wraps, soups and smoothies. (p124)

Best Bakeries

Flour Perfect scones, sandwiches, and even biscuits for your dog. (p98)

Maria's Pastry Old-school North End favorite for cannoli. (p38)

Tatte Swoonworthy pastries. (p53)

Best Local Favorites

Mike & Patty's Hole-in-the-wall serving scrumptious breakfast treats. (p83)

Trident Booksellers & Cafe Sandwiches and salads, served with a side of good books. (p100)

Best
Drinking

Despite the city's Puritan roots, modern-day Bostonians like to get their drink on. While the city has more than its fair share of Irish pubs, it also has a dynamic craft-beer movement, with a few homegrown microbreweries; a knowledge-able population of wine drinkers (and pourers); and a red-hot cocktail scene, thanks to some talented local bartenders. So pick your poison... and drink up!

Where to Drink

Boston's drinking scene is dominated by four cat-egories: dive bars, Irish bars, sports bars and a new breed of truly hip cocktail bars. Any of these types might cater to discerning beer drinkers, with local craft brews on tap or a wide selection of imported bottles. Some also morph into dance clubs as the night wears on. Boston also boasts a few sophisti-cated and semiswanky wine bars.

If you prefer caffeine to alcohol, there are scores of cute cafes and cool coffeehouses, many of which serve dynamite sandwiches and pastries.

Where to Dance

There's really only one neighborhood in Boston where the dancing goes down: the Theater District. Boylston St is the main drag, but there are venues all over this groovy 'hood. There are also clubs in Back Bay, Cambridge and Downtown.

PAUL MAROTTA/GETTY IMAGES ©

☑ Top Tips

▶ Expect to pay a cover charge of $10 to $20 at clubs.

▶ Most clubs enforce a dress code.

▶ Check club web-sites in advance to get on a guest list.

Best Views

Top of the Hub The view from the top of the Pru is fine indeed. (p100)

Pier Six Head to Charlestown for spectac-ular harborside panora-mas. (p29)

Best Vibe

Beehive A modern-day speakeasy with music, food and drink. (p84)

Tip Tap Room (p54)

Highball Lounge Board games, creative cocktails and an infectiously hip atmosphere. (p68)

Best for Beer

Tip Tap Room A truly excellent selection of craft beers on tap. (p54)

Harpoon Brewery Tour the brewery and sample a Boston classic at the source. (p70)

Best for Cocktails

Drink Unparalleled for mixology madness. (p68)

Ward 8 Named for Boston's original cocktail. (p40)

Best for Coffee

Thinking Cup Treat yourself to a frothy hazelnut latte. (p70)

Best Sport Bars

Bleacher Bar The ultimate baseball bar. (p114)

Caffè dello Sport Join the locals sipping Campari and watching football. (p40)

Best for LGBT

Club Cafe Live cabaret, tea parties, friendly people, good times. (p100)

Best Nightclubs

Good Life Get your groove on here. (p70)

Best Local Favorites

Caffè Paradiso Do the North End thing. (p33)

Zume's Coffee House Where the townies go for coffee. (p29)

21st Amendment Beacon Hill hangout for pols and their staffers. (p54)

Lucky's Lounge Every day is Throwback Thursday at Lucky's. (p70)

Delux Cafe Experience the South End before gentrification. (p84)

Best
Entertainment

JONATHAN WIGGS/THE BOSTON GLOBE VIA GETTY IMAGES ©

Welcome to the Athens of America, a city rich with artistic and cultural offerings. With the world-class Boston Symphony Orchestra and several nationally ranked music schools, Boston is a musical mecca. The Theater District is packed with venues showcasing the city's opera, dance and dramatic prowess, while more innovative experimental theaters are in Cambridge and the South End.

Best for High Culture

Boston Symphony Orchestra The city's pride and joy. (p115)

Opera House Home of the Boston Ballet. (pictured; p70)

Best for Rock

Sinclair Great small venue for new bands. (p127)

House of Blues Where the big names play. (p115)

Best for Jazz & Blues

Red Room @ Café 939 Cool place with up-and-coming acts. (p101)

Wally's Café Old-school jazz club with nightly jam sessions. (p87)

Beehive Subterranean spot with a 1920s Paris-jazz-club vibe. (p84)

Best for Drama

American Repertory Theater Cutting-edge theater in Cambridge. (p127)

Huntington Theatre Company Boston's biggest and best-known company. (p115)

Boston Center for the Arts Multipurpose space used by dozens of small companies. (p79)

Best for Comedy

Wilbur Theatre Boston's premier comedy club. (p87)

Improv Asylum Spontaneous fun in basement digs. (p42)

☑ **Top Tips**

▶ BosTix (www.bostix.org) offers discounted tickets to theater productions citywide.

▶ The BSO (p115) offers various discounted ticket schemes, as well as a rich 'Youth & Family' program.

Comedy Studio Low-budget, cutting-edge funny stuff. (p126)

Best
Shopping

Boston is known for its intellect and the arts, so you can bet it's good for bookstores, art galleries and music shops. These days, the streets are also sprinkled with offbeat boutiques, some carrying vintage treasures and local designers. Besides to-die-for duds, indie shops hawk handmade jewelry, exotic household decorations and arty, quirky gifts. It's fun to browse, even if you don't buy.

DINA RUDICK/THE BOSTON GLOBE VIA GETTY IMAGES ©

☑ Top Tip

▶ There is no sales tax in Massachusetts on clothing up to $175.

Best for Local Wares

SoWa Open Market A weekly extravaganza of arts and crafts. (p82)

Cambridge Artists' Co-operative Artist-owned and -operated. (p127)

Best Women's Fashion

Crush Boutique Sweet clothes and on-point fashion advice. (p55)

Lunarik Fashions Handbags in every size, shape and color. (p95)

Sedurre Evening wear, lingerie, dresses and jewelry. (p43)

Best Men's Fashion

Bobby from Boston Classy selection of new and vintage duds. (p87)

Ball & Buck Good-looking gear for manly men. (pictured; p95)

Uniform Designer casual wear with hipster appeal. (p87)

Best for Boston Souvenirs

Lucy's League Look good and support the team. (p71)

Beacon Hill Chocolates Sweet treats in Boston-themed keepsake boxes. (p54)

Sault New England Carefully curated New England stuff. (p87)

Blackstone's of Beacon Hill Quirky, clever gifts with a Boston theme. (p55)

Best Independent Bookstores

Harvard Bookstore Still in the square, still independent. (p121)

Trident Booksellers Good books, good coffee, good food. (p100)

Brattle Book Shop Lose an afternoon in this antiquarian bookstore. (p71)

Raven Used Books A scholarly book browser's dream come true. (p121)

Best
For Kids

Boston is one giant history museum, the setting for many lively and engaging field trips. Cobblestone streets and costume-clad tour guides can bring to life the events that kids read about in history books, while hands-on experimentation and interactive exhibits fuse education and entertainment.

Sights & Activities

There are loads of museums and activities geared specifically to kids, while even adult-oriented sites (such as art museums) have special programs to engage younger guests. Most museums and activities are free for children aged two years and under, with reduced rates for kids under 13 years. The Museum of Fine Arts is free for kids after 3pm on weekdays and all day on weekends. The Institute of Contemporary Art is always free for kids aged 17 years and under.

Sleeping & Eating

Families are a prime target market for the tourist industry in Boston, so most hotels, restaurants and tour services will do their best to accommodate your kids. Hotels often invite children to stay free in the room of their paying parent. Also, look for children's menus and high chairs in most restaurants, and changing tables in museums and other public facilities.

DAVID L. RYAN/THE BOSTON GLOBE VIA GETTY IMAGES ©

☑ Top Tip

▶ Kids aged 11 and under ride the T for free; older kids pay half price.

Best Kid Museums

New England Aquarium Explore the most exotic of natural environments under the sea. (p58)

Boston Children's Museum Hours of fun climbing, constructing and creating. Especially good for kids aged three to eight. (pictured; p66)

Museum of Science More opportunities to combine fun and learning than anywhere else in the city. (p36)

Harvard Museum of Natural History Almost as good as the zoo,

Boston Duck Tours

with room after room of stuffed animals. (p123)

Best Adventures

Spectacle Island Family-friendly facilities (and beach) in the Boston Harbor Islands. (p73)

New England Aquarium Whale Watch Whale sightings are practically guaranteed. (p66)

Best Tours for Kids

Boston Duck Tours Kids of all ages can drive the boat on the Charles River. Bonus: quacking is encouraged. (p148)

Boston by Foot Offers the only child-centered tour of the Freedom Trail. (p148)

Urban AdvenTours Rents kids' bikes, helmets and trailers. (p37)

Best Parks & Playgrounds

Boston Common Contains a huge playscape with swings, jungle gyms and all the rest. (p46)

Public Garden Swan boats on the lagoon are perfect for little tykes. (p52)

Charles River Esplanade The Stoneman Playground is a picturesque riverside spot with separate areas for different ages. (p98)

Best Cool Stuff

Prudential Center Skywalk Observatory The view from above. (p98)

Mapparium The view from inside the earth. (p98)

Best Eating for Kids

Quincy Market This big food court will satisfy the pickiest palate. (p68)

Pizzeria Regina Classic pizza in the heart of the North End. (p38)

Mr Bartley's Burger Cottage Good old-fashioned burgers with all (or none) of the trimmings. (p125)

Best
Museums

Don't let a rainy day get you down. Boston is packed with world-class museums that will keep you entertained and educated...and dry.

LUNAMARINA/GETTY IMAGES ©

Best Art Museums

Museum of Fine Arts
Boston's premier venue for art, spanning multiple centuries and the entire globe. (p106)

Institute of Contemporary Art Sometimes spectacular and sometimes strange, but always stimulating. (p60)

Isabella Stewart Gardner Museum An exquisite Venetian palazzo packed with art. (p108)

Harvard Art Museums
Three fabulous museums under one roof. (p123)

Best Science Museums

New England Aquarium
All the creatures of the sea and shoreline. (p58)

Museum of Science
Hundreds of exhibits and experiments to thrill your inner scientist. (p36)

Harvard Museum of Natural History Glass flowers, stuffed animals and more. (p123)

MIT Museum From holograms to robots, explore how the world of science works. (p126)

Best History Museums

Boston Tea Party Ships & Museum An interactive museum that allows visitors to participate in revolutionary events. (pictured; p64)

Old State House Authentic artifacts and interesting exhibits, especially focusing on the Boston Massacre. (p64)

USS Constitution Museum Learn all about a sailor's life in 1812 and the history of the US Navy. (p25)

Museum of African American History
Rotating exhibits highlighting Boston's African-American history. (p53)

Old South Meeting House Discover key moments in Boston history at the birthplace of the Boston Tea Party. (p64)

Best
Spectator Sports

MARCIO SILVA/500PX ©

Boston is fanatical about sports. And why not, with four professional sports teams – the Bruins, Celtics, Patriots and Red Sox – all piling up championships in recent years?

Baseball

After more than eight decades of heartbreaking near misses, the Boston Red Sox finally won baseball's World Series in 2004 and again in 2007 and 2013. The 2013 victory was especially sweet, as it occurred at home. The Red Sox play from April to September in Fenway Park (p110), the oldest US ball park.

Football

Five-time Super Bowl champions (2002, 2004, 2005, 2015 and 2017), the New England Patriots play at Gillette Stadium, 32 miles south of Boston in Foxborough. The regular season runs from late August to late December.

Ice Hockey

Stanley Cup winners in 2011, the Boston Bruins play ice hockey at TD Garden (p42) from mid-October to mid-April. College hockey is also huge, with the Harvard, Boston College and Boston University teams earning the devotion of spirited fans.

Basketball

The Boston Celtics have won more championships than any other NBA team, most recently in 2008. From October to April they play at TD Garden (p42).

Best Annual Sporting Events

Boston Marathon One of the country's most prestigious marathons takes place on Patriots' Day. (pictured; p102)

Head of the Charles Regatta Spectators line the Charles River in mid-October to watch the world's largest rowing event.

Beanpot Tournament Rivalries come out in full force when local college hockey teams compete at this annual event in February.

Hub on Wheels In September, this citywide bicycle ride starts at City Hall Plaza and offers three scenic routes of varying lengths.

Best
For Free

Boston can be an expensive city, but it only takes a bit of research to entertain yourself for free. Here are some options for culture vultures and history buffs with empty pockets. If you're hungry or thirsty, we've got a little something for you too.

DIEGO GRANDI/SHUTTERSTOCK ©

Free Tours

Freedom Trail National Park Service rangers lead free tours departing from Faneuil Hall. (p65)

Black Heritage Trail Free walking tour, free history lesson. (p53)

Harvard University Free student-led historical tours. (p118)

Free Art & History

Boston Public Library Free internet access, free guided tours, free books (but you have to give them back). (p90)

Massachusetts State House Free admission, free tours. (p52)

Charlestown Navy Yard Free tour of the USS *Constitution*. (p24)

Bunker Hill Monument Free view from the top (but you have to climb up there). (pictured; p27)

Free Parks & Gardens

Public Garden Stop and smell the roses. (p52)

Rose Kennedy Greenway Walk the labyrinth for free. (p65)

Mt Auburn Cemetery Free garden walks, artistic headstones and views from Washington Tower. (p124)

Charles River Esplanade Free riverside strolling. (p98)

Free Museums

Institute of Contemporary Art Free admission every Thursday after 5pm. Free admission for families on the last Saturday of the month. (p60)

Boston Children's Museum Almost free admission ($1) on Friday evenings after 5pm. (p66)

Free Eating & Drinking

Falafel King Free falafel samples! (p66)

Harpoon Brewery You'll pay for the tour but tastings are free. (p70)

Free Entertainment

Hatch Memorial Shell Free summer concerts along the Charles River Esplanade. (p101)

Shakespeare on the Common Free outdoor theater. (p49)

Harvard Square Free music by buskers. (p120)

Best Historic Tours

Freedom Trail The city's best revolutionary sites. (p130)

Black Heritage Trail Learn about Boston's abolitionist movement. (p53)

Best **History**

For all intents and purposes, Boston is the oldest city in America – and you can hardly walk a step over her cobblestone streets without stumbling upon some historic site.

Best Historic Pubs & Restaurants

Warren Tavern George Washington drank here. (p29)

Union Oyster House JFK was a regular back in the day. (pictured; p68)

Last Hurrah Omni Parker House's bar evokes Old Boston. (p70)

Best Freedom Trail Sites

Old State House Interpreting the genesis of the American Revolution. (p64)

Granary Burying Ground Final resting place for patriots and rebels. (p52)

Massachusetts State House The original 'hub of the solar system'. (p52)

Bunker Hill Monument Climb to the top for 360-degree views. (p27)

Best Gravesites

King's Chapel Burying Ground John Winthrop, first governor of the Massachusetts Bay Colony. (p64)

Granary Burying Ground Paul Revere, the fearless rider and patriot. (p52)

Mt Auburn Cemetery Henry Wadsworth Longfellow, the poet who retold American history. (p124)

Worth a Trip

The legacy of JFK is ubiquitous in Boston. The official memorial to the 35th president is the **John F Kennedy Library & Museum** (Columbia Point; www.jfklibrary.org; 9am-5pm; adult/child $14/10; T JFK/UMass) – a fitting tribute to his life and legacy.

In the suburb of Brookline, the **John F Kennedy National Historic Site** (83 Beals St; www.nps.gov/jofi; 9:30am-5pm daily mid-May–Aug, Wed-Sun Sep & Oct; free; T Coolidge Corner) occupies the modest house that was JFK's birthplace and boyhood home. Matriarch Rose Kennedy's narrative sheds light on the family's life.

Best
Tours

Best Walking Tours

Freedom Trail Foundation (www.thefreedomtrail.org; adult/child $14/8; [icon]; [T] Park St) This educational nonprofit group leads excellent tours of the Freedom Trail, broken up into bite-sized portions (eg Boston Common to Faneuil Hall, North End etc). Frequent departures from Boston Common and Faneuil Hall make this a convenient option. Tour guides are in period costume, for whatever that's worth.

Boston by Foot (www.bostonbyfoot.com; adult/child $15/10; [icon]) This fantastic nonprofit organization offers 90-minute walking tours, with neighborhood-specific walks and specialty theme tours, like the Hub of Literary America, the Dark Side of Boston, and Boston by Little Feet – a kid-friendly version of the Freedom Trail.

Best Trolley Tours

Old Town Trolley (www.trolleytours.com/boston; 200 Atlantic Ave, Long Wharf; adult/child $75/40; [T] Aquarium) Tour around the city, hopping on and off all day long. Save up to 50% when you book online. This ticket also includes admission to the Old State House and a short harbor cruise, as well as a $10 discount at the Boston Tea Party Ships & Museum.

Beantown Trolley ([phone icon] 617-720-6342; www.brush-hilltours.com; adult/child $40/20; [clock] tours 10am, 12:30pm & 3pm May-Oct) Take a two-hour tour of the city on these red-colored trolleys, with 15-minute photo breaks at Copley Sq and the USS *Constitution*. The price includes a harbor cruise from the New England Aquarium or admission to the Mapparium.

Best Boat Tours

Boston Duck Tours ([phone icon] 617-267-3825; www.bostonducktours.com; adult/child $39.50/27; [icon]; [T] Aquarium, Science Park, Prudential) These ridiculously popular tours use WWII

amphibious vehicles that cruise the downtown streets before splashing into the Charles River. The 80-minute tours depart from the Museum of Science, the Prudential Center or the New England Aquarium. Reserve ahead.

Codzilla (www.bostonharborcruises.com/codzilla; 1 Long Wharf; adult/child $29/25; [clock] hours vary May-early Oct; [T] Aquarium) 'Boating' may not be the proper word to describe this activity, which takes place on a 2800HP speedboat that cruises through the waves at speeds of up to 40mph. Painted like a shark with a big toothy grin, the boat has a unique hull design that enables it to do the ocean version of doughnuts. Warning: you will get wet.

Survival Guide

Before You Go   **150**

When to Go 150
Book Your Stay 150

Arriving in Boston   **151**

From Logan International Airport 151
From Manchester Airport 151
From TF Green Airport 151

Getting Around   **151**

Bicycle (Hubway) 151
Boat 151
Bus 151
Metro (the T) 152
Taxi 152

Essential Information   **152**

Electricity 152
Money 152
Public Holidays 153
Telephone 153
Tourist Information 153
Travelers with Disabilities 154
Visas 154

Survival Guide

Before You Go

When to Go

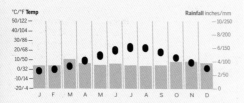

°C/°F **Temp**
50/122 —
40/104 —
30/86 —
20/68 —
10/50 —
0/32 —
-10/14 —
-20/-4 —

Rainfall inches/mm
— 10/250
— 8/200
— 6/150
— 4/100
— 2/50
— 0

J F M A M J J A S O N D

➡ **Spring (Apr–May)**
Mild weather accompanied by blooming magnolias and lilacs. Historic reenactments and marathon madness on Patriots' Day.

➡ **Summer (Jun–Aug)**
Hot and humid; locals head for the beach. Fireworks and fun on Independence Day.

➡ **Fall (Sep–Nov)** Cool, crisp air and colorful leaves. Streets are once again filled with students.

➡ **Winter (Dec–Mar)**
Cold and snow-covered, the season starts festively with Christmas activities, but lasts too long.

Book Your Stay

Useful Websites

Lonely Planet (lonely planet.com/usa/boston/hotels) Includes reviews and booking service.

Inn Boston Reservations (www.innbostonreservations.com) Studios and apartments for rent in Boston's best neighborhoods.

Boston Green Tourism (www.bostongreentourism.org) Up-to-date listings of ecofriendly hotels.

Boston Luxury Hotels (www.bostonluxuryhotels.com) Individualized service for upscale travelers.

Best Budget

HI-Boston (www.boston hostel.org) Centrally located hostel with stellar activities lineup.

40 Berkeley (www.40berkeley.com) Basic, recently renovated budget South End digs.

Best Midrange

Irving House at Harvard (www.irvinghouse.com) Spacious, well-kept B&B near Harvard campus.

Oasis Guest House (www.oasisguesthouse.com) Converted brownstone with simple rooms.

Best Top End

Newbury Guest House (www.newburyguesthouse.com) Comfortable B&B on Boston's most fashionable shopping street.

Verb Hotel (www.theverbhotel.com) Trendy music-themed hotel opposite Fenway Park.

Omni Parker House (www.omnihotels.com) Classic 19th-century hotel, right on the Freedom Trail.

Arriving in Boston

From Logan International Airport

➡ Silver-line bus (free) to South Station, then free transfer to the T (Boston's metro/subway system).

➡ Blue-line subway ($2.25 to $2.75) to central Boston; free shuttle from airport to Airport T station.

➡ Water shuttle to Boston waterfront ($9.25 to $12); free shuttle from airport to ferry dock.

➡ Taxi $25 to $30.

From Manchester Airport

➡ Located one hour north of Boston

➡ Hourly shuttle to Boston's Logan Airport operated by Flight Line Inc (www.flightlineinc.com).

From TF Green Airport

➡ Located one hour south of Boston.

➡ Massachusetts Bay Transportation Authority (MBTA) commuter rail to Back Bay or South Station ($12).

Getting Around

Bicycle (Hubway)

➡ The Hubway (www.thehubway.com) is Boston's bike-share program, offering 1600 bikes for short-term loan.

➡ Purchase a temporary membership at any bicycle kiosk, then pay by the half-hour for bike use (free under 30 minutes). Return the bike to any station in the vicinity of your destination.

➡ There are 185 Hubway stations around town; check the website for locations.

Boat

➡ The MBTA runs the F4 ferry – also known as the **Inner Harbor Ferry** (www.mbta.com; 1-way $3.50) – between Long Wharf and Charlestown Navy Yard.

➡ Boston Harbor Cruises (www.bostonharbor cruises.com) offers seasonal ferry service from Long Wharf to the Boston Harbor Islands.

➡ Boston Harbor Cruises Water Taxi (www.bostonharborcruises.com/water-taxi) makes runs from Long Wharf to the airport and other waterfront destinations.

Bus

➡ The MBTA (www.mbta.com) operates bus routes, with schedules posted on its website and at some bus stops along the routes.

➡ The standard bus fare is $2, or $1.70 with a Charlie Card. If you're transferring from the T on a Charlie Card, the bus fare is free.

➡ The silver line, a so-called 'rapid' bus, services the airport on its SL1 route. The fare is $2.75 ($2.25 with a Charlie Card).

Metro (the T)

➡ The MBTA (www.mbta. com) operates the USA's oldest subway (metro) system, known locally as the 'T'. There are four lines – red, blue, green and orange – radiating from the principal downtown stations: Downtown Crossing, Government Center, Park St and State.

➡ Buy a paper fare card ($2.75 per ride) at any station or a Charlie Card ($2.25 per ride) at designated stations. (Request a Charlie Card from the attendant before adding value at the machine.)

➡ Tourist passes with unlimited travel (on subway, bus or water shuttle) are available for periods of one day ($12) or one week ($21.25).

➡ Kids under 12 ride free.

➡ The T operates from approximately 5:30am to 12:30am. Schedules vary by line; see the website for complete details.

Taxi

➡ Cabs are plentiful but expensive. Rates are determined by the meter, which calculates miles.

➡ Expect to pay about $15 to $20 between most tourist points within the city limits, without much traffic.

Essential Information

Electricity

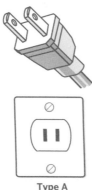

Type A
120V/60Hz

Type B
120V/60Hz

Money

Automatic Teller Machines ATMs are ubiquitous; most charge a fee (at least $2.50 per withdrawal) if your account is with a different bank.

Changing Money Change foreign currency for US dollars at Logan International Airport.

Credit Cards Major credit cards – especially Visa and MasterCard – are accepted at most hotels, restaurants, gas stations, shops and car-rental agencies.

Tipping Members of the service industry depend on tips to earn a living.

Be sure to tip baggage handlers ($2 per bag), servers and bartenders (20% for good service), housekeeping ($5 for a weekend) and taxi drivers (10% to 15%).

Public Holidays

New Year's Day January 1

Martin Luther King Jr's Birthday Third Monday in January

Washington's Birthday Third Monday in February

Evacuation Day March 17

Patriot's Day Third Monday in April

Memorial Day Last Monday in May

Bunker Hill Day June 17

Independence Day July 4

Labor Day First Monday in September

Columbus Day Second Monday in October

Veterans Day November 11

Thanksgiving Day Fourth Thursday in November

Christmas Day December 25

Telephone

All US phone numbers consist of a three-digit area code followed by a seven-digit local number. Dial 1 + all 10 digits.

Phone Codes

Area codes Boston & Cambridge 617; suburban Boston 781; North Shore 978; South Shore 508

Country code 1 for USA

International code 011

Cell Phones

Most US cell-phone systems work on the GSM 850/1900 standard, as opposed to the GSM 900/1800 standard used throughout Europe, Australia and Asia.

Tourist Information

Boston Common Information Kiosk

(GBCVB Visitors Center; Map p50 ☑617-426-3115; www. bostonusa.com; Boston Common; ☉8:30am-5pm Mon-Fri, 9am-5pm Sat & Sun; Ⓣ Park St) Starting point for the Freedom Trail and many other walking tours.

Boston Harbor Islands Pavilion

(Map p62; www. bostonharborislands.org; Rose Kennedy Greenway; ☉9am-4:30pm mid-May–Jun & Sep-early Oct, to 6pm Jul & Aug; 🛜; Ⓣ Aquarium) Conveniently located on the Rose Kennedy Greenway.

Cambridge Visitor Information Kiosk

(Map p122; ☑617-441-2884; www. cambridge-usa.org; Harvard Sq; ☉9am-5pm Mon-Fri, to 1pm Sat & Sun; Ⓣ Harvard) Detailed information on current Cambridge happenings and self-guided walking tours.

National Park Service Visitors Center

(NPS; Map p62; www.nps.gov/bost/ faneuil-hall-vc.htm; Faneuil Hall; ☉9am-6pm; Ⓣ State)

Dos & Don'ts

➔ Do stay to the right on busy sidewalks, bike paths and subway escalators.

➔ Don't compare Boston to New York: it's irrelevant.

➔ Do chat with locals about baseball, politics or anything!

➔ Don't mimic or mock the local accent. And don't 'pahk yah cah in Hahvahd Yahd' – you'll get a ticket!

Has information about the Freedom Trail sights, with a branch office at the Charlestown Navy Yard.

Travelers with Disabilities

Boston tries to cater to those with disabilities by providing cut curbs, accessible restrooms and ramps on public buildings; but old streets, sidewalks and buildings mean that facilities are not always up to snuff.

➡ Most major museums are accessible to wheelchairs, while several museums offer special programs and tours for travelers with disabilities.

➡ Many tours use wheelchair accessible vehicles. Walking tours like the Freedom Trail are also accessible, but the historic buildings may not be.

➡ MBTA buses are accessible, but not all subway trains and stations are. See MBTA Accessibility (www.mbta.com/accessibility) for more information. Ferries to the Boston Harbor Islands are all accessible.

➡ Download Lonely Planet's free Accessible Travel guide from http://lptravel.to/AccessibleTravel.

Visas

For up-to-date information about visas and immigration, check with the US State Department (www.travel.state.gov).

Visa Waiver Program

The Visa Waiver Program (VWP) allows citizens of certain countries to enter the USA without a visa for stays of up to 90 days. The list of eligible countries is subject to continual re-examination. Under this program you must have the following:

➡ A passport that meets current US standards.

➡ A round-trip or onward ticket.

➡ Adequate funds to cover the trip.

➡ Binding obligations abroad.

Electronic Authorization

All VWP applicants must receive advance approval from the Electronic System for Travel Authorization (ESTA; https://esta.cbp.dhs.gov/esta).

➡ Register online with the Department of Homeland Security as soon as possible, and at least 72 hours before arrival.

➡ Once travel authorization is approved, your registration is valid for two years. The fee, payable online, is $14.

Visa Applications

The visa validity period depends on your home country. The actual length of time you'll be allowed to stay in the USA is determined by immigration officials at the port of entry. Visa applicants may be required to submit any or all of the following:

➡ A recent photo (2in by 2in).

➡ Documents of financial stability, or evidence that a US resident will provide financial support.

➡ Evidence of 'binding obligations' that will ensure their return home.

➡ A passport valid for at least six months beyond their intended stay in the USA.

➡ A nonrefundable $160 processing fee, plus in some cases an additional visa issuance reciprocity fee.

➡ The online DS-160 non-immigrant visa electronic application.

➡ A round-trip or onward ticket.

Behind the Scenes

Send Us Your Feedback

We love to hear from travelers – your comments help make our books better. We read every word, and we guarantee that your feedback goes straight to the authors. Visit **lonelyplanet.com/contact** to submit your updates and suggestions.

Note: We may edit, reproduce and incorporate your comments in Lonely Planet products such as guidebooks, websites and digital products, so let us know if you don't want your comments reproduced or your name acknowledged. For a copy of our privacy policy visit lonelyplanet.com/privacy.

Acknowledgements

Cover photograph: Boston Public Library, Jeffrey S Rease/500px ©

Contents photograph: Charles River Esplanade, Richard Cavalleri/ Shutterstock ©

Gregor's thanks

Sincere thanks to the many Bostonians who so generously shared their love of the city, particularly Aaron Miller at HI Boston, Dave O'Donnell at GBCVB, Joanne Chang at Myers & Chang, Ayr Muir at Clover Food Lab and Maria Cole at the National Park Service (NPS). Special thanks to fellow LP author Mara Vorhees, whose superb work on previous editions made my job immeasurably more enjoyable. Finally, hugs to my wife, Gaen, and daughters, Meigan and Chloe, for helping test-taste cannoli in the North End.

This Book

This 3rd edition of Lonely Planet's *Pocket Boston* guidebook was researched and written by Gregor Clark. The previous two editions were written by Mara Vorhees. This guidebook was produced by the following:

Destination Editors Lauren Keith, Trisha Ping **Product Editors** Ronan Abayawickrema, Kate Mathews **Assisting Editors** Nigel Chin, Charlotte Orr **Senior Cartographer** Alison Lyall **Assisting Cartographer** Julie Dodkins **Book Designer** Gwen Cotter **Cover Researcher** Marika Mercer **Thanks to** Anna Cartier, Genna Patterson, Jessica Ryan, Angela Tinson, Saralinda Turner, Tony Wheeler

Index

See also separate subindexes for:

🔀 **Eating p158**

🍺 **Drinking p159**

🎭 **Entertainment p159**

🛍 **Shopping p159**

A
accommodations 150-1
Acorn Street 53
All Saints Way 33
area codes 153
Ars Libri 79
ATMs 152

B
Back Bay 88-103, **94, 96-7**
drinking 100-1
entertainment 101
food 98-100
itineraries 89, 94-5
shopping 100, 103
sights 90-3, 98
transportation 89
Barbara Lee Family Foundation Theater 61
Beacon Hill 44-55, **50-1**
drinking 54
food 53-4
itineraries 45
shopping 54-5
sights 46-9, 52-3
transportation 45
bicycling 151
Blaxton Plaque 47

Sights **000**
Map Pages **000**

boat travel 148, 151
books 85
Boston Center for the Arts 79
Boston Children's Museum 66
Boston Common 11, 46-9, 49, 50-1
transportation 45
Boston Harbor Islands 10, 72-5, **75**
Boston Harbor Islands Pavilion 73
Boston Marathon 102
Boston Massacre 48
Boston Massacre Monument 48
Boston Public Library 11, 90-1
Boston Sculptors Gallery 79
Boston Tea Party 41, 64, 67
Boston Tea Party Ships & Museum 64
Brattle Sq 121
Brewer Fountain 47
Bromfield Art Gallery 79
Bumpkin Island 74
Bunker Hill Monument 27
Bunker Hill Museum 27-8
bus travel 151-2

C
Cambridge 116-27, **120, 122**
drinking 125-6
entertainment 126-7
food 124-5
itineraries 117, 120-1
shopping 127
sights 118-19, 123-4
transportation 117
cell phones 153
Central Burying Ground 48-9
Charles River Esplanade 98
Charlestown 22-9, **26**
drinking 29
food 24-5, 28-9
itineraries 23
sights 27-8
transportation 23
Charlestown Navy Yard 11, 24-5
children, travel with 142-3
Chinatown 76-87, **80-1**
drinking 84, 86
entertainment 86-7
food 82-4
itineraries 77
shopping 87
transportation 77
chowder 69
Citgo sign 114
clams 69

climate 150
Copp's Hill Burying Ground 36
costs 16
credit cards 152
cruises 151
currency 16
cycling, see bicycling

D
disabilities, travelers with 154
Downtown 56-71, **62**
drinking 68, 70
entertainment 70-1
food 66-8
itineraries 57
shopping 71
sights 64-6
transportation 57
drinking 138-9, see also individual neighborhoods, Drinking subindex

E
electricity 152
entertainment 140, see also individual neighborhoods, Entertainment subindex
etiquette 153

F
Faneuil Hall 65

Fenway 104-15, **112**
  drinking 114-15
  entertainment 115
  food 113-14
  itineraries 105
  sights 106-11
  transportation 105
Fenway Park 9, 110-11
ferries 151
films 85
fish 69
food 136-7, *see also individual neighborhoods*, Eating *subindex*
food trucks 125
Founders Gallery 61
Freedom Trail 130-3
free activities 146
Frog Pond 48

G
Georges Island 73
Granary Burying Ground 52-3
Grape Island 74
Great Elm Site 48

H
Harvard Art Museums 123
Harvard Hall 118-19
Harvard Museums of Science & Culture 123
Harvard Square 120-1, **120**
Harvard Yard 10, 118
highlights 8-11, 12-13
history 28, 41, 48, 67, 147
holidays 153

I
Institute of Contemporary Art 10, 60-1
Isabella Stewart Gardner Museum 11, 108-9
itineraries 14-15, 130-3, 134-5, *see also individual neighborhoods*

J
John F Kennedy Library & Museum 147
John F Kennedy National Historic Site 147

K
Kenmore Square 104-15, **112**
  drinking 114-15
  entertainment 115
  food 113-14
  itineraries 105
  sights 106-11
  transportation 105
King's Chapel & Burying Ground 64

L
LaFarge, John 92-3
Langone Park 33
language 16
Lawn on D, 71
literature 85
Little Brewster Island 74
lobster 69
local life 12-13
Lomasney, Martin 42
Longfellow House 124
Lovells Island 73
Louisberg Square 53

M
Mary Baker Eddy Library & Mapparium 98
Massachusetts Hall 118-19
Massachusetts Institute of Technology (MIT) 126
Massachusetts State House 52
Mediatheque 61
metro travel 152
Mills Gallery 79
MIT Museum 126
mobile phones 153
money 16, 152-3
Mt Auburn Cemetery 124
Museum of African American History 53
Museum of Fine Arts 8, 106-7
Museum of Science 36
museums 144

N
New England Aquarium 10, 58-9
New England Aquarium Whale Watch 66
North End 30-43, **34-5**
  drinking 40
  entertainment 42
  food 37-9
  itineraries 31, 32-3
  shopping 42-3
  sights 36-7
  transportation 31
North End Branch Library 33
North End Park 32

O
Old North Church 36
Old South Meeting House 64
Old State House 64
oysters 69

P
Paul Revere House 36
Peddocks Island 74
Prudential Center Skywalk Observatory 98
Public Garden 52
public holidays 153
Puvis de Chavannes Gallery 91

R
Robert Gould Shaw Memorial 47
Rose Kennedy Greenway 65-6

S
Sargent Gallery 91
School of Fashion Design 94
seafood 69
Shakespeare on the Common 49
shopping 141, *see also individual neighborhoods*, Shopping *subindex*
Soldiers & Sailors Monument 47
Sons of Liberty 41
South End 76-87, **78**, **80-1**
  drinking 84, 86
  entertainment 86-7
  food 82-4
  itineraries 77, 78-9
  shopping 87

transportation 77
SoWa Artists Guild 78
Spectacle Island 73
sports 145
St Leonard's Church 33
subway travel 152

T
taxis 152
telephone services 153
Thompson Island 74
time 16
tipping 16, 152-3
top sights 8-11
Tory Row 124
tourist information 153-4
tours 148, *see also* walks
transport 17, 151-2
Trinity Church 9, 92-3

U
Union Park 79
Urban AdvenTours 37
USS Cassin Young 24, 25
USS Constitution 24, 25
USS Constitution Museum 25

V
visas 16, 154

W
walks 130-5, *see also individual neighborhoods*
walking tours 148

Sights p000
Map Pages p000

Ward 8 42
Waterfront 56-71, **62-3**
drinking 68, 70
entertainment 70-1
food 66-8
itineraries 57
shopping 71
sights 64-6
transportation 57
weather 101, 150
websites 16, 150
West End 30-43, **34-5**
drinking 40
entertainment 42
food 37-9
itineraries 31
shopping 42-3
sights 36-7
transportation 31
West End Museum 38
Widener Library 119

⊗ **Eating**

A
Alden & Harlow 125
Atlantic Fish Co 99

B
Barking Crab 67-8
Bistro du Midi 100
Boston Beer Works 40
Bravo 107
Butcher Shop 84

C
Café G 109
Cafe Pamplona 121
Cambridge, 1 125
Carmelina's 39
Casa Razdora 66

Clover Food Lab (Cambridge) 124
Clover Food Lab (Downtown) 66
Coppa 82
Courtyard 99

D
Daily Catch 39

E
Earl of Sandwich 47
El Pelon 113

F
Falafel King 66
Figs 28
Flour 98

G
Galleria Umberto 38
Giacomo's Ristorante 39
Gourmet Dumpling House 82

I
Island Creek Oyster Bar 113

L
Legal Harborside 67
L'Espalier 99-100
Life Alive 124

M
Map Room Cafe 91
Maria's Pastry 38-9
Mike & Patty's 83
Mr Bartley's Burger Cottage 125
My Thai Vegan Café 84
Myers & Chang 82

N
Navy Yard Bistro & Wine Bar 28
Neptune Oyster 37
New American Café 107
No 9 Park 54

P
Paramount 53-4
Parish Café 99
Pizzeria Regina 38

Q
Quincy Market 68

R
Reef 59
Row 34 66-7

S
Salumeria Italiana 33
Sam La Grassa's 66
Scampo 39
South End Buttery 79

T
Tangierino 29
Tapestry 114
Tasty Burger 114
Tatte 53
Toro 83

U
Union Oyster House 68

W
Water Cafe 61

Y
Yankee Lobster Co 67

🍷 Drinking

21st Amendment 54

A

Alibi 40

B

Beat Brasserie 125
Beehive 84
Bin 26 Enoteca 54
Bleacher Bar 114
Brick & Mortar 126
Bukowski Tavern 100

C

Caffé dello Sport 40
Caffé Paradiso 33
Caffé Vittoria 40
Candi 86
Club Café 100-1

D

Delux Café 84
Drink 68

G

Gallows 79, 84
Good Life 70

H

Harpoon Brewery &
    Beer Hall 70
Hawthorne 115
Highball Lounge 68

J

Jacob Wirth 86

L

Last Hurrah 70
Lower Depths Tap
    Room 115

Lucky's Lounge 70

P

Pier Six 29
Polcari's Coffee 33

T

Thinking Cup 70
Tip Tap Room 54
Top of the Hub 100

W

Ward 8 40
Warren Tavern 29
Wired Puppy 134

Z

Zume's 29

🎭 Entertainment

American Repertory
    Theater 127
Berklee Performance
    Center 101
Boston Symphony
    Orchestra 115
Brattle Theatre 121
Club Passim 126
Comedy Studio 126
Cutler Majestic
    Theatre 86
Hatch Memorial
    Shell 101
House of Blues 115
Huntington Theatre
    Company 115
Improv Asylum 42
Opera House 70-1
Red Room @ Café
    939 101
Shubert Theatre 86
Simons IMAX
    Theatre 59

Sinclair 127
TD Garden 42
Wally's Café 87
Wilbur Theatre 87

🛍 Shopping

B

Ball & Buck 95
Beacon Hill
    Chocolates 54-5
Blackstone's of
    Beacon Hill 55
Bobby From
    Boston 87
Brattle Book Shop 71

C

Cambridge Artists'
    Cooperative 127
Converse 95
Crush Boutique 55

D

Daniela Corte 95

E

Eugene Galleries 55

G

Garage, The 121
Greenway Open
    Market 71
Grolier Poetry
    Bookshop 121

H

Harvard Bookstore 121

I

In-Jean-ius 43
In Your Ear 121

L

Lucy's League 71
Lunarik Fashions 95

M

Marathon Sports 103
Marika's Antique
    Shop 55

N

Newbury Comics 103
North Bennet Street
    School 42-3

O

Out of Town News 120

R

Raven Used Books 121

S

Sault New England 87
Sedurre 43
Shake the Tree 43
SoWa Farmers
    Market 82
SoWa Open
    Market 82
SoWa Vintage
    Market 82

T

Three Wise
    Donkeys 95
Trident
    Booksellers 100
Twentieth Century
    Ltd 55

U

Uniform 87

Our Writer

Gregor Clark

Gregor is a US-based writer whose love of foreign languages and curiosity about what's around the next bend have taken him to dozens of countries on five continents. Chronic wanderlust has also led him to visit all 50 states and most Canadian provinces on countless road trips through his native North America.

Since 2000, Gregor has regularly contributed to Lonely Planet guides, with a focus on Europe and the Americas. Titles include *Italy*, *France*, *Brazil*, *Costa Rica*, *Argentina*, *Portugal*, and *New England's Best Trips*, as well as coffee-table pictorials such as *Food Trails*, *The USA Book* and *The LP Guide to the Middle of Nowhere*.

Published by Lonely Planet Global Limited
CRN 554153
3rd edition – December 2017
ISBN 978 1 78657 250 9
© Lonely Planet 2017 Photographs © as indicated 2017
10 9 8 7 6 5 4 3 2
Printed in Malaysia